THAI
MADE EASY

Yui Miles

SIMPLE, MODERN
RECIPES FOR EVERY DAY

cover illustration by Jordan Amy Lee
photography by Luke Albert

quadrille

INTRODUCTION

I was born and raised in Bangkok, in a strong Thai-Chinese family where cooking and eating were always a focal point of family life. My parents cooked traditional Thai- and Chinese-inspired dishes throughout my childhood, which I helped prepare and cook from a very young age. As well as at home, we loved eating out at our local street food market.

When in Thailand you will regularly hear Thai people ask each other: '*Gin khao yung?*' which means 'Have you eaten yet?'. This is our way of saying hello, similar to 'What's up?' or 'How's it going?'. In Thai culture, food is really important in a family setting and with friends, and thus forms a focal part of our lives and general wellbeing.

When I got married and moved to the UK in 2001, I began to learn to cook more European and British food, while adding my own Southeast Asian twist. I followed my heart and passion for authentic Southeast Asian cuisine, which led to me showcasing my dishes on BBC's 2019 *MasterChef* and Channel 4's *Beat the Chef*.

Every time I visit Thailand for reunions with my friends and family, we not only cook together at home, we go out for delicious and authentic Thai street food, which has inspired many of the recipes in this book. *Thai Made Easy* will show you how easy it is to recreate beautiful Thai dishes in your own home with ingredients that can be easily sourced, whether grown locally or imported. I hope it will inspire you to create delicious Thai dishes in the comfort of your own kitchen.

Khop khun ka,

Yui

MY THAI LARDER

These are commonly used larder ingredients in Thai cooking. I've suggested easy swaps in individual recipes, where necessary.

FRESH INGREDIENTS AND SPICES

Chillies

A common chilli in Thai curry pastes, stir-fries and spicy dishes is a long red or green Thai chilli called *prik chi faa*. We also use a big, red chilli called *prik jinda* for a less spicy flavour and to garnish. Bird's eye chillies are uniquely small, thin, pointy and very spicy. They are red when mature and green when unripe. They are used in curry pastes (especially green), stir-fries, sauces and more. Thai cooking also uses dried red chillies in curry pastes and sauces, as they give a spicy, sweet and smoky flavour. Thai chilli flakes, made from pounded dried Thai chillies, are commonly used in Thai condiments, noodles and spicy salad dishes.

Chinese chives

Also known as garlic chives, these flat, tender leaves have a mild garlic flavour and can be found in Chinese supermarkets. They can usually be replaced with spring onions (scallions).

Cinnamon

Cinnamon is used as an aromatic flavouring and is a spice often used in Chinese-inspired dishes, both savoury and sweet.

Coriander (cilantro) roots

The roots from bunches of Thai coriander are often used as an aromatic, usually pounded with dried peppercorns and garlic to make a paste for stir-frying or marinating meat. If you can't find coriander roots, use stalks instead.

Coriander seeds

These tiny, aromatic seeds are used mostly in Thai curry pastes and marinades for meat. They are normally lightly toasted before use to release their fragrance.

Cumin seeds

Another dried spice that we often use in curry pastes and Indian-influenced dishes, as well as in sauces like satay sauce. They are generally toasted before use to release their aroma.

Dried peppercorns

These are often used in Thai cooking, mostly pounded with coriander (cilantro) roots and garlic to make a paste for stir-fried or marinated meat. They add a nice peppery and umami flavour.

Galangal

Widely used in curry pastes and to infuse soups, galangal should not be confused with root ginger, as they work in very different ways. You can find galangal in Asian supermarkets; buy a big batch and freeze it to keep it fresh.

Garlic

Thai garlic is a lot smaller and stronger-tasting than the Chinese garlic varieties standardly found in supermarkets, and we usually use it whole, including the skin. If you can get hold of Thai garlic, that's great, but you can simply use the garlic found in your local supermarket instead for ease.

Ginger

Fresh root ginger is often used in Southeast Asian-influenced dishes. Most ginger you see in the UK and US is mature ginger, but in Thailand you can find younger ginger too, which is tender, juicy and thin-skinned. It's often used in pickles or side dishes. Use whatever is available to you.

Lemongrass

This long, slim stalk is often used in Thai kitchens. One of the key ingredients in many curry pastes, it is a must-have ingredient in tom yum soup and is also added to some spicy salad dishes. We normally remove the tough outer leaves first, trimming off the root end and working from that end, then stopping when we reach the green part. If you can't find fresh lemongrass, some supermarkets have jarred available.

Lesser galangal

Lesser galangal, or Chinese ginger, or *kra chai* in Thai (there are many names depending on the country), is a relative of ginger with a sweet, peppery taste and a milder, more lemony flavour than ginger. Also often called finger root because of its hand-like appearance, it is commonly added to jungle curry and fish curry.

Limestone water

Nam poon daeng, or limestone water, is used in many forms of cooking, not only in Thai food but in various baked and fried foods worldwide. It is known in other parts of the world as pickling lime, slaked lime, lye water or cal. Limestone paste is used to make slaked limestone water by combining the paste and water (in a 1:20 ratio) in a jar or bottle, mixing well and waiting for 20 minutes or so. The paste will sink to the bottom and clear water will stay on top, which is then used to make fried foods extra crispy. Limestone water is also used to soak vegetables such as pumpkin and sweet potato before cooking, to prevent them from turning mushy. If you can't find limestone, use 1 tbsp bicarbonate of soda (baking soda) for every 240ml (8fl oz/1 cup) water.

Makrut limes: leaves and zest

Makrut lime leaves are used a lot in Thai dishes such as tom yum, stir-fries and in curries as a garnish. They have a central, woody stem that should be removed before use. You can buy them in Asian and other large supermarkets; I often buy a big batch and freeze them. Makrut lime zest is one of the key ingredients for many Thai curry pastes. If you can't get hold of makrut limes you can use standard lime or lemon zest instead.

Shallots

Baby shallots are used a lot in Thai cooking, and they are an indispensable ingredient in many curry pastes, stir-fries and soups, or when fried until crispy and used as a garnish, for extra crunch.

Star anise

This pretty, star-shaped seedpod is used in many Chinese-influenced Thai dishes, and is great in a stew or braise. The spice is often pan-toasted over a low heat to release its flavour before use.

Thai basil

In Thailand we have three main types of basil: Thai sweet basil, Thai holy basil and hairy (or lemon) basil, each used for different typical dishes:

- Thai sweet basil is the most well-known and is widely used in Thai cooking. It has a peppery, sweet taste and we add it to some curries and stir-fries towards the end of cooking.

- Thai holy basil has jagged-edged green leaves and soft, fuzzy hair on the stems and leaves. It is commonly found in the dish pad krapow and is also used in some spicy curries. If you can't find it, you can use Thai sweet basil instead.

- Hairy basil (or lemon basil) has a lemony scent that accounts for its name, and it is normally used in Thai spicy broths and curries without coconut milk.

All Thai basil varieties can be substituted with Italian basil, but the flavour will be slightly different, as Italian basil is sweeter. Thai basil has a more peppery, aniseed flavour.

Turmeric: fresh and ground

Fresh turmeric, in root form, can be found in most supermarkets and Asian supermarkets (Indian and Chinese); you can buy a big batch and store it whole in the freezer, where it will keep for months, and take out a small quantity at a time to use. Ground turmeric is often used in southern Thai cuisine and brings a gorgeous deep yellow colour as well as a peppery, mildly bitter flavour to the dish.

Young green peppercorns

Used more for accent than as a paste ingredient, these are added to some curries and stir-fry dishes. They give a spicy heat that warms the throat rather than burns the tongue. If you can't find fresh, you can use the brined version in a jar; if neither is available, leave them out altogether.

Wild betel leaves

Heart-shaped wild betel leaves, or *bai cha plu*, are sold as fresh leaves and often added to yellow or red curry, or used in a Thai snack dish called *miang kham*. Find them online or in Asian supermarkets. If you can't get hold of them, simply leave them out of the recipe.

MY THAI LARDER

WRAPPERS, NOODLES AND RICE

Spring roll wrappers
Paper-thin pastry available in packets from Asian supermarkets and some supermarkets, and perfect for Thai spring rolls.

Wonton wrappers
Square egg noodle sheets used mainly for making wonton soup and crispy wonton. Find them in Asian or large supermarkets.

Egg noodles
Made from eggs and wheat flour, in a process similar to pasta: the dough is cut into long, thin noodle shapes then portioned into nests and wound into bundles, with 6–8 nests in one bag. Fresh egg noodles can be found in Chinese supermarkets but if you can't find fresh, use dried Chinese-style noodles and cook according to the packet instructions.

Glass noodles
Clear noodles made from mung bean flour, which gives them a chewy texture. Often used to make spicy salads or stir-fries.

Rice noodles
Also called *sen lek* or pad Thai noodles, these long, thin dried rice noodles are made from rice flour. This noodle is often used for fried noodle dishes and noodle soups, as well as pad Thai.

Thai jasmine rice
A long-grain rice more or less served with every Thai meal.

Thai sticky rice / Thai glutinous rice
A stickier-textured rice than jasmine often served with spicy salads and Thai BBQ dishes, or in desserts. It needs to be soaked in cold water for a good few hours – or overnight – before it is steamed.

Riceberry
Popular in Thailand, this soft, deep-purple wholegrain rice variety is created from a cross-breed of Jao Hom Nin and Khao Dawk Mali varieties. Available from Thai grocery stores or Asian supermarkets. If you can't find it, use brown or wild rice instead.

Tapioca
Tapioca pearls are a starch made from the cassava root. Widely used in Thai desserts and snacks, they can come in large and small sizes. Tapioca is used to add texture and absorb flavours.

Vermicelli rice noodles
This very thin noodle is made from rice flour and is used widely in Asian cooking. Much thinner than rice noodles, they need very little cooking time – perfect for adding to a soup, stir-fry or salad.

CONDIMENTS

Coconut milk
Coconut milk is essential in Thai cuisine and can be used to make curries, soups, dipping sauces, smoothies, marinades, or desserts and ice cream. Available in cans or cartons. Try to buy coconut milk without binding agents so the thick part and liquid remain separate.

Dark sweet soy sauce
A Chinese-influenced sauce that is sweet and sticky and almost black, similar to Indonesian kecap manis, and normally used in some stir-fried noodle dishes such as *pad see ew* for the colour and smoky caramel flavour. Like for thin soy sauce (see opposite), look for a brand such as Healthy Boy or Lee Kum Kee.

Fish sauce
Thai food cannot be Thai food without fish sauce! Thai fish sauce is made from anchovies fermented with salt and is a must-have for the Thai kitchen. Look for a Thai brand such as Squid, Tip Pa Rod or Megachef for the best results.

Oyster sauce
Popular for use in Thai and Chinese stir-fried dishes, oyster sauce is basically made from oyster extract, sugar and salt. Packed with umami for a strong, savoury taste.

Palm sugar
Palm sugar has a mild caramel and nutty flavour and is made from the cooked sap of the coconut palm. It is sold in many forms, including blocks, nuggets, a soft version in a pot, compressed cakes and big grains. We use it a lot in curry dishes, for making sauces, dipping sauces and Thai desserts. When using palm sugar from a block in the recipes in this book, it is best to flake it with a knife, making it easier to measure and dissolve into dishes. If you cannot find it, substitute with brown sugar.

Rice vinegar
A clear vinegar used a lot in Thai cooking, often used to add a lovely sharpness of flavour to various sauces.

Shrimp paste
Another essential ingredient for making Thai curry pastes and many spicy dishes, shrimp paste has a very pungent smell when raw, but when roasted or grilled, it loses its pungency and brings a rich, savoury umami taste to a dish. Available in Asian supermarkets. Substitute with miso paste for a vegan- and vegetarian-friendly option.

Soy sauce
Also known as thin soy sauce or white soy sauce, this is used a lot in Thai and Chinese-influenced dishes. There are many kinds and brands of soy sauce, but I tend to use Amoy, Healthy Boy or Lee Kum Kee.

Sriracha sauce
The favourite sauce of Thai people! Sriracha is a sharp, sour, tangy, spicy, garlicky sauce that goes so well with many Thai dishes, including Thai crispy omelette, crispy fried egg and more. It can also be used in stir-fry sauces or marinades.

Sweet chilli sauce
You might hear Thai people called this sauce *nam jim gai* ('sauce for grilled chicken') because it goes so well with grilled chicken and other grilled meat. Made from red chillies, white vinegar, sugar and salt, it is sweet, savoury and tangy with a little bit of heat. It is also perfect for serving with many Thai dishes, such as spring rolls and sweetcorn fritters. See page 172 for homemade.

Sweet plum sauce
Or in Thai *nam jim buoy*, this Chinese-style plum sauce is a light brown, sweet and sour dipping sauce that is perfect with deep-fried dishes such prawn toast.

Tamarind paste
Tamarind is a dried pod-like brown legume that is made into a sour concentrated paste or pulp that is commonly found in the Thai kitchen; it gives earthy acidity to Thai cooking.

Thai Chilli Jam
Or *nam prik pao* in Thai, this is another versatile, umami-rich condiment used in Thai cooking. We like to add this to tom yum, or to a spicy salad or stir-fry. It made from roasted garlic, shallots, dry red chillies, shrimp paste and dry shrimp, blended together and seasoned with palm sugar, tamarind paste and fish sauce. You can buy it in most Asian supermarkets and online.

USEFUL EQUIPMENT

Bamboo steamer
Typically used in Chinese and Thai-Chinese cooking, for example in steamed fish and dim sum dishes. I also use a bamboo steamer when cooking Thai sticky rice.

Fine hand-held grater (Microplane)
Especially handy for grating garlic and ginger.

Julienne peeler
A useful tool for creating perfect long, thin matchsticks from vegetables and fruit, in particular carrots, cucumber, kohlrabi and papaya.

Knives
In the Thai kitchen we use a large chef's knife for chopping, cutting and bashing ingredients, such as garlic and chillies. Also typically used in Thai-Chinese food preparation is a meat cleaver, a very versatile tool that is used for everything from dicing meat to bashing and chopping herbs and vegetables. We also use a small, specially shaped carving knife for creating decorative fruit and vegetables.

Pestle and mortar
An essential piece of equipment in any Thai kitchen and the tool of choice when preparing so many Thai dishes, including curry pastes.

Rice cooker
In Thai households, where we eat rice every day, there is *always* a rice cooker and it is the hero of the kitchen. Not only a time-saver, it also always achieves perfect results.

Wok
A very versatile piece of cookware for preparing a variety of Thai dishes, this is perfect for stir-frying, deep-frying and – with a bamboo steamer placed over it – steaming.

Thai
SNACKS

PRAWN TOAST

(KHANOM PANG NA KUUNG)

Makes 20—24 pieces

Cooking time: 25 minutes

200g (7oz) raw peeled prawns (shrimp)

2 spring onions (scallions), finely chopped

1 tbsp soy sauce

1 tsp sugar

1 tbsp sesame oil

1 egg yolk

2 garlic cloves, minced

1 tbsp ground white pepper

5—6 slices of stale bread, each cut into 4 triangles

1 tbsp sesame seeds (a mixture of black and white)

100ml (3½fl oz) vegetable oil

To serve
Thai sweet chilli sauce (see page 172 for homemade) or sweet plum sauce

This is a delicious snack from my childhood. If you have any stale bread, don't throw it away! Make this dish instead.

Chop the prawns (shrimp) until coarsely minced (ground) (or use a food processer), then add to a bowl with the spring onions (scallions), soy sauce, sugar, sesame oil, egg yolk, garlic and pepper. Mix well.

Spread the mixture thinly and evenly over each bread triangle, then sprinkle sesame seeds on top of each.

Heat the vegetable oil in a deep frying pan over a medium heat and shallow-fry the toasts upside down to start with, for 3 minutes, then turn them over and fry until cooked and golden, another 2—3 minutes.

Serve with sweet chilli or plum sauce.

Easy Swap
You can also use minced (ground) pork or chicken instead of prawns.

CHICKEN SATAY

(SATAY GAI)

Serves 2 as a sharing plate

Cooking time: 35 minutes, plus marinating

2–3 boneless, skinless chicken breasts or thighs, cut into long strips about 2 x 4.5cm (¾ x 1¾in)

2–3 tbsp vegetable oil, for frying

For the marinade

2 tbsp ground toasted peanuts, or creamy peanut butter

2 tbsp soy sauce

1 tbsp palm sugar or brown sugar

2 tbsp curry powder

1 tsp ground turmeric

1 tsp ground white pepper

1 tsp ground cumin seeds

1 tbsp grated fresh ginger

5–6 tbsp coconut milk

1 tbsp Sriracha sauce (optional)

2–3 tbsp fresh pineapple juice (optional; it helps tenderize the chicken)

For the satay sauce

240ml (8fl oz/1 cup) coconut milk

1 tbsp Thai red curry paste (see page 179)

1–2 tbsp palm sugar or brown sugar

1–2 tsp salt

1 tbsp curry powder

To serve

1 quantity ar jard (see page 174)

You will need 5–6 bamboo skewers, soaked in water for 10 minutes

These delicious satay skewers are made of chicken marinated in an aromatic peanut sauce, then grilled. Thai chicken satays are often served with satay sauce and ar jard; we take a chicken skewer and pour over some satay sauce, then take a bite and follow with the ar jard, which is so light and refreshing. Usually enjoyed with cucumber and chillies to munch on, too.

In a mixing bowl, combine the ingredients for the marinade. Place the chicken strips in the marinade, cover and refrigerate for at least 30 minutes; overnight is best.

Preheat a griddle pan to a medium-high heat and use a brush or paper towels to coat the surface of the pan with a little oil.

Weave the chicken onto the skewers, then griddle for 5–8 minutes on each side, turning and using a pastry brush to brush the leftover marinade on the chicken on the second turn.

Meanwhile, for the satay sauce, put all the ingredients along with any leftover marinade into a small saucepan. Place over a medium heat and stir until the sauce nice and thick. Taste the sauce: it should be sweet, salty and creamy.

Serve the chicken skewers with the satay sauce and ar jard.

Easy Swap

You can also use pork, beef or prawns (shrimp) instead of chicken.

KING PRAWNS IN BLANKETS

(KUUNG HOM PA)

Makes about 10

Cooking time: 15 minutes

8–10 raw king prawns (shrimp),
  peeled and deveined

Pinch each of salt and ground
  white pepper

Handful of fresh egg noodles
  or cooked spaghetti

120ml (4fl oz/½ cup) vegetable oil

Handful of shredded cabbage,
  to garnish

**For the sweet chilli
  Sriracha sauce**

1 tbsp Sriracha sauce

1 tbsp Thai sweet chilli sauce (see
  page 72 for homemade)

1 tbsp finely diced cucumber

This snack is super-easy to make and delicious; perfect for a party or get-together. _Hom pa_ means 'wrap in the blanket'.

Dry the prawns (shrimp) with paper towels, then season with the salt and pepper. To make your 'blanket', take a prawn and wrap a noodle or piece of spaghetti around it, covering it entirely. Repeat with the remaining prawns.

Mix the sauce ingredients together in a small bowl and set aside.

Heat the oil in a deep frying pan over a medium heat and shallow-fry the prawns for 2–3 minutes on each side, until golden and crisp. Transfer to paper towels and serve with the sweet chilli Sriracha sauce for dipping and the shredded cabbage on the side.

CALAMARI WITH CRISPY GARLIC

(PLA MUEK CHUUP PANG TORD)

Serves 2 as a sharing plate

Cooking time: 25 minutes

4 squid tubes, cleaned and sliced into rings

100g (3½oz) panko breadcrumbs

Vegetable oil, for frying

5–6 garlic cloves, finely chopped

For the batter

4 tbsp plain (all-purpose) flour

1 tbsp cornflour (cornstarch)

1 tsp dried chilli flakes

Pinch each of salt and ground white pepper

120ml (4fl oz/½ cup) soda water or cold water

To serve

Coriander (cilantro) leaves

Sliced cucumber

Thai sweet chilli sauce (see page 172 for homemade) or Sriracha sauce

This Thai version of calamari with crispy garlic is a moreish finger food to share for a snack or starter. Serve with Thai sweet chilli sauce or Thai-style plum sauce for dipping.

For the batter, mix the dry ingredients in a bowl, then stir in the water until combined and smooth.

Add the squid rings and mix to make sure that every bit is coated.

Place the panko breadcrumbs on a plate, then transfer the squid onto the breadcrumb plate and coat the rings on both sides.

Heat enough vegetable oil for shallow-frying in a deep frying pan over a medium heat. When the oil is hot (add a pinch of breadcrumbs to the oil – if they lightly sizzle the oil is ready) add the calamari and fry until golden on both sides. Remove with a slotted spoon and transfer to paper towels to drain.

In a small frying pan, heat 3–4 tablespoons of oil and fry the garlic until crisp and golden. Remove with a slotted spoon and transfer to a paper towel to drain.

Place the calamari on a plate and top with the fried garlic. Scatter with coriander (cilantro) and serve with cucumber on the side and either sweet chilli sauce or Sriracha for dipping.

Easy Swap

If you can't find panko, you can use regular breadcrumbs – the end result just won't be as flaky.

CRISPY PORK PARCELS

(MOO GRA BUANG)

Makes 12–16

Cooking time: 25 minutes

200g (7oz) minced (ground) pork

2 spring onions (scallions), finely chopped

2 tbsp finely diced carrot

2 garlic cloves, minced

1 tsp ground white pepper

1 tbsp soy sauce

1 tbsp oyster sauce

6–8 spring roll wrappers (12 x 12cm/5 x 5in)

120ml (4fl oz/½ cup) vegetable oil

To serve
Sriracha sauce or sweet plum sauce

Another delicious snack I can never get enough of in my house. Crispy on the outside thanks to the the spring roll wrapper but soft and flavourful in the centre.

Place the pork in a mixing bowl, add the spring onions (scallions), carrot, garlic, pepper, soy sauce and oyster sauce, and mix well.

Cut a spring roll wrapper diagonally to give 2 triangles, then add about 1 teaspoon of filling mixture to one half of the triangle sheet. Use your thumb or a spoon to press the mixture down and fold the spring roll wrapper in half. Use a small brush to dampen the edges of the wrapper with water, allowing you to close and seal. Press down firmly to get rid of excess air. You should have a small triangular parcel.

Heat the oil in a deep frying pan over a medium heat and shallow-fry your parcels for about 2–3 minutes, then turn over and cook on the other side for another minute or two. Remove from the oil and drain on paper towels.

Serve with Sriracha or sweet plum sauce.

Easy Swap
You can swap out the pork for the same weight of minced (ground) tofu or prawns, depending on what you have available.

PORK PATTIES

(MOO KORN)

Moo korn, or Thai minced (ground) pork patties, are my childhood favourite – my mum would often make them for an after-school snack. Use mashed tofu in place of pork for a vegetarian option (you will also need to replace the fish sauce with soy sauce and use vegetarian oyster sauce).

Makes 12 small patties

Cooking time: 30 minutes

1 tbsp finely chopped coriander (cilantro) root or stalks

2 garlic cloves, finely chopped

1 tbsp white peppercorns (or ground white pepper)

150g (5oz) minced (ground) pork or chicken

2 tbsp cornflour (cornstarch)

2 tbsp oyster sauce

3 tbsp finely chopped onion

2 tbsp finely chopped spring onions (scallions)

1 tbsp fish sauce

2–3 tbsp vegetable oil

For the crispy garlic
100ml (3½fl oz) vegetable oil

6–9 garlic cloves, finely chopped

To serve
Sriracha or Thai sweet chilli sauce (see page 172 for homemade)

Pound the coriander (cilantro) roots or stalks, garlic and peppercorns together in pestle and mortar until it becomes a fine paste.

Add the pork, cornflour (cornstarch), oyster sauce, onion, spring onions (scallions) and fish sauce to a mixing bowl. Add the coriander paste and mix well.

Form the mixture into ping-pong-sized balls and press them down a little in the middle to form a patty shape. Set aside in the fridge for 15 minutes to firm up.

Meanwhile, to make the crispy garlic, heat the 100ml (3½fl oz) vegetable oil in a frying pan over a medium heat, add the garlic and stir with a spatula until it turns crisp. Take off the heat and transfer with a slotted spoon to a small bowl. The garlic will continue to turn more golden and crisp as it cools.

Wipe the pan clean, then add the 2–3 tablespoons of oil and place over a medium heat. Add the pork patties and fry for about 5–8 minutes, then turn them over to cook on the other side. Continue cooking, turning them until they are evenly browned and cooked through. Transfer to paper towels before serving topped with the crispy garlic, and Sriracha or sweet chilli sauce for dipping.

Easy Swap
For a leaner version, use minced (ground) chicken or turkey in place of the pork.

SWEETCORN FRITTERS

(TOD MAN KHAO POD)

Makes 12

Cooking time: 30 minutes

1 x 160g (6oz) can of sweetcorn, drained

Handful of green beans, finely chopped

Handful of Thai basil leaves, roughly chopped

4 makrut lime leaves, central woody stem removed, finely sliced

1 tbsp Thai red curry paste (see page 179 for homemade)

4 tbsp plain (all-purpose) flour

1 tbsp cornflour (cornstarch)

50ml (1¾fl oz) soda water or cold water

2 tbsp soy sauce

1 tsp brown sugar or palm sugar

Pinch each of salt and ground white pepper

150ml (5fl oz/2/3 cup) vegetable oil

To serve
Thai sweet chilli sauce (see page 172 for homemade)

My childhood is written all over this well-known Thai snack. You can also add meat such as minced (ground) chicken or a can of tuna.

Add the sweetcorn, beans, basil, lime leaves, curry paste, flour and cornflour (cornstarch) to a large mixing bowl and mix well. Add the water a little at a time and stir until fully combined.

Season with the soy sauce, sugar, salt and pepper. Mix well.

Heat the oil in a deep frying pan over a medium-high heat, then use an ice-cream scoop or tablespoon to scoop the fritter mixture gently into the hot oil, about 4 or 5 scoops at a time. Fry for around 3 minutes, then carefully turn the fritters over and cook the other side for the same time, until golden and crisp.

Remove with a slotted spoon and transfer to paper towels to drain, then serve with sweet chilli sauce for dipping.

Easy Swap
If you can't get hold of makrut lime leaves, use the zest of 1 lime or lemon instead.

You can use fresh sweetcorn in place of canned, if you prefer.

ONE-BITE MONEY BAGS
(KHANOM THUNG THONG)

Makes 10–12

Cooking time: 25 minutes

250g (9oz) minced (ground) pork
  or chicken

2 garlic cloves, finely chopped

½ medium onion, finely chopped

½ carrot, finely chopped

1 spring onion (scallion), finely
  chopped, plus 2–3 green parts
  only, sliced lengthwise

2 tbsp oyster sauce

2 tbsp soy sauce

1 tsp ground white pepper

1 egg white

10–12 wonton wrappers

220ml (7½fl oz) vegetable oil

Thai money bags are a traditional savoury snack. Thai people often eat these on special occasions like New Year gatherings or birthdays, as we believe they bring you luck and money.

In a bowl, mix the minced (ground) pork with the garlic, onion, carrot and chopped spring onion (scallion), then season with the oyster sauce, soy sauce and pepper. Add the egg white and mix well.

Soak the green spring onion strips in just-boiled water for a few minutes, then rinse and place in cold water. Rinse again, then dry using paper towels. Set aside.

Separate out your wonton wrappers. Put one wrapper on the palm of your non-dominant hand and add about 1 teaspoon of the filling. Gather the edges of the wrapper around the filling and gently squeeze the edges together at the top to enclose. Repeat the process to use up all the wrappers and filling.

Tie a spring onion strip around the top of each money bag to secure it.

Heat the oil in a deep frying pan over a medium heat until hot enough to fry (my tip is to dip a chopstick in the hot oil: if it makes a sound and creates bubbles it means the oil is hot enough).

Add your money bags to the pan one at a time (you will need to do this in two batches), and fry for 5–6 minutes, until they turn golden and crisp. Remove with a slotted spoon and drain on paper towels briefly before serving.

VEGETABLE SPRING ROLLS
(POR PHER PAK)

Makes 12

Cooking time: 30 minutes

1 small packet (50–80g/2–3oz) glass noodles

280ml (9½fl oz) vegetable oil, plus 2 tbsp

2 garlic cloves, finely chopped

⅛ sweetheart cabbage, finely sliced

1 small carrot, julienned

2 tbsp soy sauce

2 tbsp fish sauce

2 tbsp oyster sauce

1 tsp sugar

1 egg, roughly beaten

3 spring onions (scallions), finely sliced

2 handfuls of beansprouts

Pinch of ground white pepper

12 medium (20cm/8in) spring roll wrappers

To serve

Ar jard, for dipping (see page 174)

Easy and delicious Thai spring rolls to make in no time at home. We often have this for a snack or party food and they are perfect for cooking in a big batch and freezing for later. Use this recipe as a base and adapt it to suit your tastes: minced (ground) pork, chicken or prawns (shrimp) are all good additions.

Put the glass noodles into a heatproof bowl, add boiling water to cover and leave to soak for 10 minutes. Drain and cut into bite-sized pieces.

Heat the 2 tablespoons of vegetable oil in a pan over a medium heat, add the garlic and stir well for 1–2 minutes, then add the cabbage, carrot and chopped glass noodles and cook for another 5–6 minutes.

Add the soy sauce, fish sauce, oyster sauce and sugar and stir well. Add the egg and stir until the egg mixes with the other ingredients and absorbs the moisture. Let cook for a couple of minutes, then add the spring onions (scallions) and beansprouts. Season with the pepper, take off the heat and set aside.

Separate out the spring roll wrappers and lay them on a flat surface, with points facing towards you. Add about 1 tablespoon of filling to the first wrapper. Starting with the point closest to you, roll the wrapper over the filling. Next, fold both side points into the middle to seal the ends of the spring roll, then continue to roll the spring roll away from you so the filling is enclosed. Add a little water to the inside edge of the far point to seal. Repeat the process until you have used up all the wrappers and filling. Cover with a damp dish towel to prevent them drying out.

Heat the 280ml (9½fl oz) vegetable oil in a wok or deep frying pan over a medium-high heat. Fry 4–5 spring rolls at a time for about 3–4 minutes on each side. Once cooked, place them on paper towels to drain, then serve with ar jard for dipping.

Easy Swap

If you can't get hold of spring roll wrappers, try using filo (phyllo) pastry instead. Place 2–3 layers on top of each other for each roll.

sharing
PLATES

SPICY FRUIT SALAD

(TUM PHOL LA MAI)

Serves 2

Cooking time: 15 minutes

Handful each of grapes,
  strawberries, satsuma
  segments, pineapple
  or peach, chopped

1 apple, cored and chopped

3–4 cherry tomatoes, halved

½ carrot, grated

4–5 green beans, halved

Handful of roasted cashews or
  peanuts (optional)

For the dressing

2 tbsp fish sauce or soy sauce

1 tbsp brown sugar, maple syrup
  or honey

Juice of 1 lime (2–3 tbsp)

1–2 tbsp dried chilli flakes, to taste

This tasty and healthy dish is very popular in Thailand. It is similar to Thai papaya salad (see page 77) but is made with seasonal fruits instead of green papaya. Perfect for a light meal, side dish or snack.

To make the dressing, whisk the ingredients together in a small bowl.

In a large bowl, combine all the fruits, tomatoes, carrot and beans. Drizzle the dressing over and toss to combine. If you like, add roasted cashews or peanuts and mix them in well before serving.

Easy Swap
You can use any seasonal fruits you prefer, such as nectarine, cherries and/or gooseberries.

SPICY GLASS NOODLE SALAD

(YUM WOON SEN)

Serves 2

Cooking time: 20 minutes

150g (5oz) glass noodles

1 tbsp vegetable oil

120g (4¼oz) minced (ground) pork

120g (4¼oz) raw peeled prawns (shrimp)

½ onion, finely sliced

2 spring onions (scallions), finely sliced

Handful of cherry tomatoes, halved

2 tbsp roasted and salted peanuts

Handful of coriander (cilantro), roughly chopped

Crispy garlic (optional; see page 29)

For the sauce

4 bird's eye chillies, finely chopped

Juice of 2 limes (3–4 tbsp)

1 tbsp brown sugar

3 tbsp fish sauce

1 tbsp Thai chilli jam (nam prik pao)

This Thai-style salad is spicy, tangy and salty. It's so easy to make: simply cook your glass noodles as the base and add your preferred protein and vegetables. Great served warm or chilled.

Put the glass noodles in a heatproof boil, pour boiling water over them to cover and leave for 6–8 minutes. Drain, transfer to a mixing bowl, add the oil and mix well.

Blanch the pork and prawns (shrimp) in boiling water for a couple of minutes until cooked, breaking up any lumps of pork as they form, then drain and add to the noodles.

Mix the sauce ingredients together in a separate bowl and taste, adding more lime juice, fish sauce or sugar if needed; it should be sour, salty and a little sweet.

Pour the sauce into the noodle bowl, mix well, then add the onion, spring onions (scallions), tomatoes, peanuts, coriander (cilantro) and crispy garlic, if using, and mix again.

Easy Swap

The traditional sauce uses a Thai chilli jam called *nam prik pao*, but you can leave it out or use your favourite chilli oil instead.

SPICY TUNA SALAD
(YUM TUNA)

Serves 2

Cooking time: 15 minutes

Handful of shredded cabbage

½ white onion, finely sliced

¼ cucumber, finely sliced

Handful of mint leaves, finely chopped

2 spring onions (scallions), finely sliced

120g (4¼oz) drained canned tuna

For the sauce

1 tsp finely chopped red chilli

1 tbsp soy sauce or fish sauce

Juice of 1 lime (2–3 tbsp)

1 garlic clove, finely sliced

1 tsp sugar

This salad is my dad's signature dish that I would like to share with you. Healthy and light but tasty and full of Thai flavour, this is also super-quick to prepare.

Mix the sauce ingredients together in a bowl and set aside.

Toss together the cabbage, onion, cucumber, mint and spring onions (scallions) in a large bowl, then arrange on a serving plate.

Scatter the tuna on top of the salad then pour over the spicy sauce. Toss lightly then serve.

SALMON WATERFALL SALAD

(NAM TOK SALMON KROB)

Serves 4

Cooking time: 35 minutes

6–8 tbsp plain (all-purpose) flour

Pinch each of salt and ground white pepper

120ml (4fl oz/½ cup) milk or 1 beaten egg

6–8 tbsp panko breadcrumbs

3 salmon fillets, about 350g (12oz) in total, sliced into long pieces

100ml (3½fl oz) vegetable oil

For the sauce

2 garlic cloves, finely chopped

2–3 Thai red chillies, finely chopped

1 tsp dried chilli flakes (optional)

1 tbsp Thai chilli jam (nam prik pao), optional

1–2 tsp toasted ground rice (see page 169)

1–2 tbsp fish sauce

Juice of 1–2 limes (about 4 tbsp)

1–2 tbsp palm sugar or brown sugar

To serve

1 baby gem lettuce, finely shredded

Handful of coriander (cilantro) leaves

½ large cucumber, finely sliced

Handful of mint leaves

2–3 baby shallots, finely sliced

Light, crispy salmon with a classic spicy Thai flavour, this is my take on *nam tok* (Thai-style spicy salad). The key to this dish is using toasted ground rice as it adds a nutty, smoky flavour.

Combine all the sauce ingredients in a bowl, adding the fish sauce, lime juice and sugar to taste.

Mix the flour and salt and pepper together and spread out in a shallow bowl or tray. Place the milk or beaten egg into another bowl or tray, and the panko breadcrumbs into a third.

Dredge the salmon pieces through the flour using one hand (your 'dry' hand), then transfer to the milk or beaten egg tray, use your other hand (your 'wet' hand) to move the salmon around the liquid until coated, then transfer to the breadcrumbs. Use your dry hand to sprinkle breadcrumbs all over the salmon pieces and make sure they are well coated. Transfer all the breadcrumbed salmon to a clean plate, ready to fry.

Heat the oil in a large frying pan over a medium heat, then shallow-fry the salmon pieces until golden and crisp on both sides. Transfer to paper towels to drain.

To serve, add the shredded lettuce and cucumber to a plate, top with the crispy salmon then drizzle over some spicy sauce. Top with coriander (cilantro), mint and shallot.

Easy Swap

Use whatever fish you have available; sea bass and sea bream work particularly well.

PORK TOAST
WITH AR JARD

(KA NOM PANG NHA MOO KUB AR JARD)

Serves 4–5

Cooking time: 20 minutes

200g (7oz) minced (ground) pork

2 tbsp fish sauce

1 tbsp soy sauce

1 tbsp oyster sauce

1 tbsp ground white pepper

1 spring onion (scallion), finely
 chopped

5 slices of stale bread, each cut
 into 4

Small handful of coriander
 (cilantro) leaves

1–2 red chillies, finely sliced

100ml (3½fl oz) vegetable oil

2 eggs, beaten

To serve
Ar jard (see page 174) or Thai
 sweet chilli sauce (see page 172
 for homemade)

This is a snack from my childhood that I love so much! My mum would make this for me when I got home from school – just enough to fill my tummy while waiting for dinner time.

Mix the pork, fish sauce, soy sauce, oyster sauce, pepper and spring onion (scallion) together in a mixing bowl.

Spoon about 1 tablespoon of the pork mixture on top of each piece of bread, spread it evenly then lightly press a few coriander (cilantro) leaves and chilli slices on top of each.

Heat the oil in a frying pan over a medium heat. Lightly dip the pork-topped side of the squares in the beaten egg then transfer to the hot oil, pork side down. Fry for a couple of minutes then turn over and continue to fry until crisp and cooked through. Transfer to paper towels to drain.

Serve with ar jard or sweet chilli sauce.

Easy Swap
You can replace the pork with minced (ground) chicken or prawns (shrimp).

MINCED PORK SALAD

(LAAB MOO)

Serves 2

Cooking time: 20 minutes

100ml (3½fl oz) water

250g (9oz) minced (ground) pork

Juice of 1 lime (2–3 tbsp)

3–4 tbsp fish sauce

2–3 tsp Thai chilli flakes

2 tsp toasted ground rice (see page 169)

3–4 baby shallots, finely sliced

Handful of green beans, finely chopped

4–5 baby tomatoes, roughly chopped

Handful of mint leaves

To serve

Thai sticky rice (see page 168), optional

Mint leaves (optional)

4–5 baby gem lettuces, divided into leaves

This tasty northern/Isan-style spicy, salty and sour minced (ground) pork salad is served in lettuce leaves, but you could also serve it with Thai sticky rice.

Heat the water in a small saucepan until boiling. Add the pork and use a ladle or spatula to break up any lumps of meat, then stir well until cooked through.

Reduce the heat to low, then add the lime juice, fish sauce, chilli flakes and toasted ground rice, and mix well. Taste it; it should be salty, sour, nutty and spicy. Remove from the heat and add the shallots, green beans, tomatoes and mint leaves. Mix well.

Serve with sticky rice and lettuce leaves on the side for people to construct their own, or place the leaves on a platter and scoop some of the laab moo into each leaf. Garnish with mint, if you like.

Easy Swap

You can use minced (ground) chicken instead of pork. For a plant-based version use minced tofu in place of the pork and use a vegetarian fish sauce, or soy sauce.

SPICY SWEETCORN SALAD

(SOM TUM KHAO POD)

Serves 2

Cooking time: 15 minutes

1 large sweetcorn cob, husks removed

Handful of peanuts

1 tbsp desiccated (dried shredded) coconut

1–2 garlic cloves, roughly chopped

1–2 Thai bird's eye chillies or small red chillies, roughly chopped

1 carrot, julienned

Handful of green beans, halved

Handful of cherry tomatoes, halved

Juice of 1 lime (2–3 tbsp), or more to taste

2–3 tbsp fish sauce

1 tsp palm sugar or brown sugar

Handful of finely shredded cabbage or lettuce

A light but tasty, spicy salad that is perfect on its own or served with BBQ meat.

Cook the sweetcorn in a pan of boiling, salted water for 8–10 minutes. Drain, then cook on a griddle pan or BBQ until nice and charred all over. Slice the kernels off the cob and set aside.

Put the peanuts and coconut in small frying pan over a medium heat and toast for a few minutes. Set aside.

Pound the garlic and chillies in a pestle and mortar then tip into a bowl and add the carrot, beans, tomatoes, lime juice, fish sauce and sugar.

Add the grilled sweetcorn, cabbage or lettuce, and the toasted peanuts and coconut. Mix well before serving.

Easy Swap
You can use drained canned sweetcorn in place of fresh – simply skip the first step of the method.

BETEL LEAF WRAPS

(MIANG KHAM)

Makes 1 sharing plate for 4

Cooking time: 20 minutes

2 tbsp small dried shrimp

4 tbsp toasted peanuts or cashews

4 tbsp desiccated (dried shredded) coconut or dried coconut shavings

1 lime, cut into small pieces (leave the skin on)

4 tbsp finely diced, peeled ginger

2 baby shallots, chopped

2 bird's eye chillies, finely chopped

10–15 wild betel leaves

For the miang sauce

1 tbsp finely chopped galangal

1 tbsp finely chopped lemongrass (white part nearest to the roots only)

1 baby shallot, finely chopped

1 tbsp shrimp paste

1 tbsp fish sauce

150g (5oz) palm sugar

2 tbsp toasted desiccated (dried shredded) coconut

Miang kham translates as 'one bite wrap', from *miang* (food wrapped in leaves) and *kham* (a bite). It's a sharing platter snack that originated in the northern part of Thailand, originally using pickled tea leaves (called *miang* in the northern Thai language). It is usually eaten with family and friends and is also popular in the central region of Thailand.

First make the miang sauce. Pound the galangal, lemongrass and shallot in a pestle and mortar until it turns into a rough paste, then add the shrimp paste and mix well.

Add the fish sauce and sugar to a saucepan over a medium heat, then add the paste and stir gently until it has a gravy-like consistency. Add the coconut, take off the heat and transfer to a small serving bowl; it will thicken up more as it cools.

One ingredient at a time, lightly toast the dried shrimp, peanuts or cashews and coconut in a dry frying pan. Tip onto a plate to cool.

Assemble everything on a big plate by placing the sauce bowl in the middle and working your way around, adding bowls of the toasted peanuts or cashews, coconut and shrimp paste, the lime pieces, ginger, shallots, chillies and wild betel leaves.

To serve, pick up a wild betel leaf in your hand, then spoon a combination of the ingredients onto the leaf with the sauce on top. Wrap and put into your mouth in one bite.

Easy Swap
If you can't find betel leaves, use any Chinese green leaves such as choy sum, pak choi (the green part) or even baby gem lettuce leaves.

street
FOOD

STIR-FRIED PRAWNS WITH HOLY BASIL AND CHILLI

(PAD KRAPOW GUUNG)

Serves 2

Cooking time: 20 minutes

Vegetable oil, for cooking

2–3 garlic cloves, finely chopped

3–4 Thai bird's eyes chillies, finely sliced

160g (5½oz) raw peeled king prawns (shrimp)

Handful of green beans, chopped

1 tbsp soy sauce

1 tbsp oyster sauce

2 tsp fish sauce

1 tsp brown sugar

Couple of handfuls of holy basil or Thai basil

2 duck eggs (or chicken eggs, but duck eggs have a lovely orange yolk)

Ground white pepper

To serve

Steamed rice

Sliced cucumber

Deep-fried basil (optional)

Nam pla prik (see page 175)

Here is my version of what has to be the most popular and classic Thai street food dish. You can also replace the prawns (shrimp) with pork, chicken, beef or tofu, and feel free to add other veggies such as onion, carrot or red pepper. The stunning sauce acts as a glaze as the prawn mixture cooks over the high heat. The trick is to have all the ingredients prepped before you start cooking.

Heat a large wok over a high heat. Drizzle in 2 tablespoons of oil, then add the garlic and chilli and stir-fry until the garlic starts to turn golden, about 2–3 minutes. Add the prawns (shrimp) and continue cooking over a high heat until the prawns are 80% cooked. Add the green beans then the soy sauce, oyster sauce and fish sauce, and cook and stir until the sauce begins to caramelize, about 1 minute. Add the sugar and stir well.

Add the basil and stir until wilted, about 20 seconds, then add pepper to taste. You can add a splash of water if the sauce becomes a little dry. Take off the heat.

Heat 2–3 tablespoons of oil in a small frying pan over a high heat, and add the eggs, one at a time for crispy edges. Cook until the edges of the white become crispy but the yolk is still runny.

Serve the stir-fry with rice and cucumber, topped with a fried egg, some deep-fried basil, if you like, and the nam pla prik dipping sauce on the side.

Easy Swap

If you can't find either holy or Thai basil, use Italian basil. Note that Italian basil is sweeter.

RAILWAY FRIED RICE

(KHAO PAD ROD FAI)

Serves 2

Cooking time: 30 minutes

2 tbsp vegetable oil

2 garlic cloves, finely chopped

1 onion, finely sliced

220g (8oz) cold cooked rice

1 tbsp fish sauce

1 tbsp light soy sauce

1 tbsp dark soy sauce

½ tsp sugar

1 tbsp Sriracha sauce

1 large tomato, cut into wedges

2 handfuls of shredded kale

2 eggs

2 spring onions (scallions), finely
  chopped

Handful of coriander (cilantro),
  roughly chopped

Ground white pepper

To serve

Nam pla prik (see page 175)

Lime wedges

Sliced cucumber

Spring onions (scallions), optional

This dish evokes childhood memories of going on holiday for a long weekend. We travelled by train, and a vendor came on to the train selling food. This is one of the dishes they sold, and which I happily shared with my sister.

Heat the oil in a non-stick frying pan and, once it is medium-hot, sauté the garlic quickly for 20 seconds until it turns golden and crispy. Quickly add the onion and stir, followed quickly by the cooked rice. Stir rapidly to break down any rice clumps.

Add the fish sauce, soy sauces, sugar and Sriracha and stir quickly to combine the flavours. Add the tomato and kale and give it a quick stir to combine.

Push your fried rice to one side, add the eggs to the clear space and mix them through the rice. Once it is all combined, remove the pan from the heat and sprinkle over the spring onions (scallions), coriander (cilantro), and pepper to taste.

Serve with nam pla prik and lime wedges, with some cucumber and spring onion on the side, if you like.

DRUNKEN NOODLES

(PAD KEE MAO)

Serves 2

Cooking time: 25 minutes

115g (4oz) dried flat rice noodles (or you can use vermicelli rice or egg noodles)

4–5 tbsp vegetable oil

3–4 large dried chillies

3 garlic cloves, finely chopped

3–4 fresh red chillies

1 onion, finely sliced

150g (5oz) boneless, skinless chicken breast or thighs, cut into bite-sized pieces

Handful of green beans, chopped into lengths of about 3cm (1¼in)

4–5 baby corns, sliced in half lengthwise

2–3 vines of fresh baby green peppercorns (optional)

2 handfuls of Thai basil

For the sauce

2 tbsp soy sauce

2 tbsp oyster sauce

1 tbsp fish sauce

2 tbsp brown sugar

In Thai cuisine, this hot and spicy stir-fried rice noodle dish is a popular and well-known Thai street food. *Kee mao* means 'drunken' and several theories exist around the name. Most people say that it refers to the spiciness it tends to have, making diners drink heavily to combat the heat. Some say it's because it is an excellent hangover cure, others that it is so hot that the eater has to be drunk to be able to stand it!

Soak the noodles in cold water for about 10 minutes to soften them up. Rinse, transfer to a bowl, add 1 tablespoon of the oil and mix well. Set aside.

Mix the sauce ingredients together in a small bowl and set aside.

Drizzle the remaining 3–4 tablespoons of oil into a frying pan over a medium heat, add the dried chillies and quickly fry for 30 seconds. Remove from the pan and set the chillies aside (leaving the oil behind in the pan).

Add the garlic to the pan and quickly stir, then add the fresh red chillies and onion. Stir for 30 seconds, until fragrant. Add the chicken and mix well for a couple of minutes, then add green beans and baby corn and mix well. Add the drained noodles and the sauce and toss to mix, then add 2–3 tablespoons of water, if needed, to loosen the sauce. Add the peppercorns, if using, and Thai basil, then toss and remove from the heat.

Top with the reserved fried chillies and serve.

Easy Swap

If you can't find fresh young peppercorns you can use young peppercorns in brine, or simply leave them out.

You can use Italian basil in place of the Thai basil.

SOUR AND SPICY SOUP WITH PRAWNS

(TOM YUM KUUNG)

Serves 2

Cooking time: 30 minutes

1 thumb-sized piece of fresh galangal (about 5cm/2in), thickly sliced

5 Thai bird's eye chillies (or less, to taste), roughly chopped

4–5 baby shallots, peeled and halved

2 lemongrass stalks, cut into 4–5cm (1½–2in) lengths

8 raw king prawns (shrimp), ideally shell-on

1 tbsp vegetable oil (if making prawn shell stock)

About 500ml (17fl oz) water (or chicken stock if not making prawn shell stock; see method)

4–5 cherry tomatoes, halved

1 tbsp tamarind paste

2 tbsp fish sauce

1 tbsp Thai chilli jam (or chilli oil)

120g (4¼oz) mushrooms, halved if large

6–8 makrut lime leaves, central woody stem removed, torn in half

Juice of 2 limes (3–4 tbsp)

To garnish
Coriander (cilantro) leaves

Roughly chopped spring onion (scallion)

To serve
Perfect jasmine rice (page 168)

A well-known, delicious, spicy and sour soup originating in central Thailand and full of fragrant spices and herbs. It's addictively delicious. This is my version, inspired by my mum's recipe.

Using a rolling pin or pestle and mortar, bruise the galangal, chillies, shallots and lemongrass.

Peel the prawns (shrimp), leaving the head and tail on. Use the prawn shells to make a stock by heating the vegetable oil in a large saucepan and adding the shells. Stir well until the shells are cooked and toasted and have released their natural oil. Add the water and boil for about 10 minutes, then strain through a sieve (strainer) into a bowl. Discard the shells and return the stock to the pan. (If not using shell-on prawns, make the dish using chicken stock.)

Bring the stock to the boil over a medium heat then add the bruised galangal, chillies, lemongrass and shallots, along with the tomatoes. Give it a quick stir.

Season with the tamarind paste, fish sauce and Thai chilli jam, and mix well.

Add the prawns, mushrooms and lime leaves and give it a quick stir. Once the prawns are cooked take the pan off the heat and stir in the lime juice. Garnish with coriander (cilantro) and spring onion (scallion). Serve straight away with steamed jasmine rice.

Easy Swap
If you can't find fresh galangal, use a jarred version or replace with ginger, if you can't get hold of either.

Substitute the makrut lime leaves with the zest of 2 lemons or limes, if needed.

STIR-FRIED NOODLES WITH PORK

(PAD SEE EW)

Serves 2

Cooking time: 30 minutes

3 tbsp vegetable oil

3 garlic cloves, finely chopped

250g (9oz) boneless pork fillet, finely sliced

Handful of kale, Chinese cabbage or pak choi

2 eggs

2 tbsp light soy sauce

1 tbsp dark sweet soy sauce (see page 14)

1 tbsp oyster sauce

1 tbsp white sugar

Ground white pepper

For the noodles

150g (5oz) dried flat rice noodles

1 tbsp dark sweet soy sauce (or use dark soy sauce)

1 tbsp vegetable oil

To serve

Prik nam som (see page 171)

This is another popular Thai street food dish that I have adapted for you to have a go with at home – it's a delicious and easy stir-fried noodle dish to be enjoyed with family and friends.

Put the rice noodles in a heatproof bowl, add boiling water to cover and leave to soak for about 15 minutes. Drain, transfer to a mixing bowl and add the dark sweet soy sauce and oil, mix well and set aside.

Heat the 3 tablespoons of oil in a frying pan or wok over a medium-high heat, then add the garlic, stir well and add the pork, quickly mixing it in.

Add the prepared noodles and toss well. Add the kale, Chinese cabbage or pak choi, and stir to combine everything.

Over a fairly high heat, make a small well on one side of the pan and break the eggs into it. Leave them for a couple of minutes, then start to break the eggs with a spoon to make a soft scramble. Once the eggs are nearly cooked, mix them through the noodles.

Add the soy sauces, oyster sauce and sugar to season, then mix well and sprinkle with pepper. Serve with prik nam som (see page 171).

Easy Swap

This is a great dish for using up what you have in the fridge. You can replace the rice noodles with egg or glass noodles, use chicken in place of pork (boneless, skinless chicken thighs or breast work best), and add whatever greens you have that need using up.

SWEET AND SOUR SPICY NOODLE STIR-FRY

(PAD MEE KORAT)

Serves 2–3

Cooking time: 30 minutes

180g (6oz) dried flat rice noodles

200g (7oz) pork belly (side), cut into 1.5cm (⅔in) chunks

4 baby shallots, finely sliced

2 tbsp fish sauce

1 tbsp salted soybeans

2 tbsp palm sugar

2 tbsp tamarind paste

2 tbsp dark sweet soy sauce (see page 14)

1 tbsp Thai chilli flakes

240ml (8fl oz/1 cup) water

4–5 spring onions (scallions) or Chinese chives, chopped into 4cm (1½in) lengths

100g (3½oz) beansprouts

To serve

Lime wedges

Thai chilli flakes (optional)

This is a spicy rice noodle stir-fry that traditionally uses pork belly although you can also use chicken or tofu. Super-easy and delicious – think of it as a spicier version of pad Thai.

Soak the rice noodles in a large bowl of cold water for 2–3 minutes, then drain and cover with a lid or foil.

Heat a frying pan or wok over a medium heat, add the pork pieces and keep stirring until they brown and release fat. Remove from the pan (leaving the rendered fat in the pan), transfer to a plate and set aside.

Add the shallots to the pan and stir until fragrant, then make the sauce by adding the fish sauce, salted soybeans, sugar, tamarind, dark sweet soy and chilli flakes. Add the water and mix until combined.

Add the drained rice noodles to the pan and stir well, then reduce the heat to low and occasionally stir the noodles until they have absorbed the sauce; add more water if the sauce becomes too dry. Taste your noodles: they should be sweet, sour, spicy and salty, so add more sugar, tamarind or fish sauce to taste, if needed.

Add the pork back to the pan, followed by the spring onions (scallions) or Chinese chives, and the beansprouts, and toss everything together.

Serve with lime wedges and extra chilli flakes, if you like.

CRYING TIGER

(SEUA RONG HAI)

Serves 2

Cooking time: 15 minutes, plus marinating and resting

½ quantity nam jim jaew (see page 170)

1 rump (sirloin) steak, about 250g (9oz)

1 tbsp vegetable oil

Coriander (cilantro), to garnish

To serve
Thai sticky rice (see page 168) or Spicy papaya salad (see page 77), optional

Also known as 'weeping tiger', this is basically a marinated steak served with the spicy dipping sauce nam jim jaew, an amazing combination of spicy, sweet and sour flavours. You can use other cuts of steak, such as sirloin or T-bone, or replace it with spatchcocked chicken or pork chops.

Scoop out about 1 tablespoon of nam jim jaew sauce and coat the steak. Leave to marinate at room temperature for about 30 minutes.

Heat a frying pan or griddle pan over a medium heat. Rub the oil all over the steak then add it to the hot pan and pan-fry for 8–10 minutes, turning it halfway through, for medium-rare.

Remove the steak to a board and leave to rest for 5–6 minutes before slicing with a sharp knife. Once sliced, spoon the remaining sauce on top and garnish with some coriander (cilantro). Serve with Thai sticky rice or Spicy papaya salad, if you like.

STIR-FRIED NOODLES WITH PRAWNS

(PAD THAI KUUNG SOD)

Serves 2

Cooking time: 25 minutes

200g (7oz) dried flat rice noodles

3–4 tbsp vegetable oil

2–3 garlic cloves, finely chopped

2 shallots, finely sliced

200g (7oz) raw peeled king prawns (shrimp)

4–5 tbsp toasted peanuts, roughly crushed in a pestle and mortar

2 eggs

Handful of beansprouts

4 spring onions (scallions) or Chinese chives, chopped into lengths about 4cm (1½in)

For the sauce

2 tbsp brown sugar

4 tbsp palm sugar (or use more brown sugar)

4 tbsp tamarind paste

2–3 tbsp fish sauce

125ml (4¼fl oz) water

To serve

1–2 tsp Thai chilli flakes (optional)

1 lime, cut into wedges

Handful of beansprouts (optional)

Pad Thai is a delicious stir-fried flat rice noodle dish, commonly served as a street food in Thailand. This is my easy cook-at-home version – stir-fried rice noodles with prawns (shrimp) in sweet sticky tamarind sauce. What's not to enjoy?

Soak the rice noodles in cold water in a large bowl for about 10 minutes, until softened. Drain and set aside.

Cook all the sauce ingredients in a small saucepan over a medium heat until the sugar dissolves and the sauce thickens to a gravy consistency (add a little more water if needed). Take off the heat.

Heat 2 tablespoons of oil in a frying pan or wok over a medium heat, add the garlic and shallots and stir for a minute. Add the prawns (shrimp) and stir until cooked, then tip onto a plate and set aside.

Add the drained rice noodles to the same pan and stir well, then add 2–3 tablespoons of your sauce and 1 tablespoon of crushed peanuts and toss. Taste the noodles: they should be sweet, sour and salty – add more sugar, tamarind or fish sauce if you like.

Move the noodles to one side of the pan, add about 1 tablespoon of oil and then the eggs. Leave the eggs to cook for a few minutes before mixing them through the noodles. Add the cooked prawns back to the pan, stir well then add the beansprouts along with the spring onions (scallions) or Chinese chives.

Divide between plates, drizzle with the remaining sauce and sprinkle with the remaining crushed peanuts and some chilli flakes. Serve with a wedge of lime and extra beansprouts on the side, if you like.

Easy Swap
You can use glass noodles in place of rice noodles if you prefer.

CRISPY NOODLES WITH GRAVY

(RAD NHA MEE KROB)

Serves 2

Cooking time: 30 minutes

1 tbsp vegetable oil

2 garlic cloves, finely chopped

200g (7oz) boneless pork fillet, or boneless, skinless chicken thighs or breast, finely sliced

1 carrot, sliced into rounds

Handful of broccoli florets

Handful of cauliflower florets

Handful of baby corn, halved lengthwise

2 pak choi, cut into bite-sized pieces

Handful of sugar snap peas

For the crispy noodles

500ml (17fl oz) vegetable oil

200g (7oz) fresh egg noodles

For the gravy

2 tbsp oyster sauce

1 tbsp fish sauce

1 tbsp soy sauce

1 tbsp sesame oil

1 tbsp sugar

1 tsp ground white pepper

1 tbsp fermented bean or miso paste

3 tbsp cornflour (cornstarch)

240ml (8fl oz/1 cup) chicken stock or water

To serve

Prik nam som (see page 171)

Crispy egg noodles with a Chinese-style pork gravy, this is a comforting dish inspired by Chinese chow mein that Thai people have adopted and adapted to our own tastes.

Combine the gravy ingredients, except the chicken stock, in a bowl and set aside.

For the crispy noodles, heat the oil in a large, deep pan or wok over a medium heat. Divide the noodles into 2 nests then add one nest to the hot oil. Use a spatula to separate the noodles a little then flip them. Cook until both sides turn crispy and golden, then transfer to paper towels to drain. Repeat with the second nest of noodles.

For the pork or chicken and vegetables, heat the oil in a frying pan or wok over a high heat. Add the garlic and cook until crisp and golden, then add the pork or chicken, mix well and cook, stirring, for 10 minutes. Add all the vegetables in order, with the longest to cook first, stirring well.

Add the gravy mixture, mix well and let it simmer for a few minutes to thicken. Add the chicken stock or water and simmer for a few more minutes, adding a little more water if the gravy is too thick.

To serve, place the crispy noodles on serving plates, then spoon over the meat, vegetables and gravy. Serve immediately with prik nam som on the side.

Easy Swap

Feel free to cook the noodles according to the packet instructions, rather than frying them. You can also use flat rice or vermicelli noodles for this dish. If you buy egg noodles in a big portion, you can freeze some to use another time. Simply portion them up and freeze in a zip-lock bag. Defrost for 10–15 minutes before using.

CRISPY PANCAKES

(KHANOM BUANG YUAN)

Serves 4

Cooking time: 30 minutes, plus resting

150g (5oz) Asian rice flour

2 tbsp cornflour (cornstarch)

1 tbsp ground turmeric

1 x 400g (14oz) can of coconut milk

Pinch of salt

125ml (4¼fl oz) water or limestone water (see page 10)

3–5 tbsp vegetable oil

120g (4¼oz) cooked shredded chicken or pork, or peeled prawns (shrimp)

½ red (bell) pepper, finely sliced

1 carrot, finely sliced into matchsticks

2–3 spring onions (scallions), finely sliced

100–120g (3½–4oz) beansprouts

2 baby gem lettuces, leaves separated

To serve
Ar jard (see page 174)

This is inspired by a Vietnamese crispy chicken pancake, but I've given it a tasty Thai twist and served it with Thai ar jard dipping sauce. Please give it a go at home – you will want this for breakfast, brunch and dinner after you've tried it!

Mix the rice flour, cornflour (cornstarch), turmeric and coconut milk together in a mixing bowl. Add the salt, then add the water a little at a time until you have a batter with the consistency of single (light) cream. Leave to rest for at least 20 minutes.

Heat about 2 tablespoons of the oil in a large non-stick frying pan or wok over a medium heat. When the oil is hot, pour a ladle of the pancake mixture into the pan and swirl it evenly over the pan.

When the pancake is looking cooked around the edges, on one half add a little of the shredded chicken or pork, or prawns (shrimp), (bell) pepper, carrot, spring onions (scallions) and beansprouts. By this point the pancake should be cooked underneath – fold the empty half over the filling.

Put a plate on top of your pan then carefully invert the pan – your pancake should easily come off onto your plate.

Repeat to make 3 more pancakes, heating 1 tablespoon of oil for each.

To serve, cut a bite-sized piece of pancake, place in a lettuce leaf, add some ar jard and enjoy in one bite.

Easy Swap
If you use limestone water (see page 10) instead of water, the pancakes stay crispy for longer, but it's not essential.

For a plant-based pancake, swap the meat for tofu or mushrooms.

Do note, I have specified Asian rice flour here as it differs from free-from varieties of rice flour that you find in the baking aisle. You can find Asian rice flour in Asian supermarkets or in the world food aisle of large supermarkets.

PINEAPPLE FRIED RICE

(KHAO PAD SAPPAROD)

Serves 2

Cooking time: 20 minutes

½ small pineapple

2 tbsp vegetable oil

3 garlic cloves, finely chopped

200g (7oz) raw peeled prawns (shrimp)

1 white onion, sliced

½ red (bell) pepper, finely diced

½ carrot, cut into 5mm (¼in) dice

50g (1¾oz) fresh or frozen peas

2 tbsp soy sauce

1 tbsp fish sauce

1 tbsp sugar

1 tbsp curry powder

1 tsp ground turmeric

220g (8oz) cold cooked rice

50g (1¾oz) roasted cashews

Pinch of ground white pepper

2 spring onions (scallions), thinly sliced

To serve

Nam pla prik (see page 175)

Thai pineapple stir-fried rice, or *khao pad sapparod*, served with Thai chilli dipping sauce, or nam pla prik, takes me back to a holiday in Thailand when I ordered this dish at a beach restaurant and it came served in a pineapple in place of a plate.

Using a small, sharp knife, cut away the flesh of the pineapple then use a spoon to scoop it out. Wash the shell and dry with paper towels, then set aside. Cut away and discard the core from the flesh, then cut the flesh into 1.5cm (⅔in) cubes.

Heat the oil in a large frying pan, add the garlic and cook, stirring, for 1 minute until golden. Add the prawns (shrimp) and stir-fry for 2–3 minutes. Add the onion, (bell) pepper, carrot and peas and cook, stirring, for 2 minutes.

Season with the soy sauce, fish sauce and sugar, then stir in the curry powder and turmeric and mix well.

Add the cooked rice and stir-fry for a few minutes, using a spatula to separate the grains, until the rice is completely coated in the sauce. Add the pineapple flesh and cashews and stir well for a few minutes.

Spoon into the pineapple shell to serve, sprinkled with white pepper and spring onions (scallions), and with nam pla prik dipping sauce on the side.

Easy Swap

You can use canned instead of fresh pineapple, if needed. And of course you can simply serve this dish on a plate, rather than in a pineapple!

STICKY THAI CHICKEN WINGS

(PEAK KAI YANG)

Serves: 4

Cooking time: 40 minutes, plus marinating

500g (1lb 2oz) chicken wings

For the marinade
3 coriander (cilantro) roots (or use a handful of stalks instead)

4 garlic cloves, chopped

1 tbsp black peppercorns

2 tbsp soy sauce

1 tbsp fish sauce

1 tbsp Sriracha sauce

1 tbsp oyster sauce

1 tbsp sugar

To serve
3 spring onions (scallions), finely chopped

Sliced red chilli

Perfect served with som tum (see page 77) and Thai sticky rice (see page 168), as well as nam jim jaew or nam pla prik (see pages 170 and 175).

Pound the coriander (cilantro) roots or stalks, garlic and peppercorns to a fine paste in a pestle and mortar. Transfer to a bowl, add the soy sauce, fish sauce, Sriracha, oyster sauce and sugar, and mix well. Add the chicken wings to the bowl and, using your hands, work the marinade into the chicken.

Transfer everything to a large zip-lock bag and leave to marinate for at least 30 minutes, or ideally overnight in the fridge.

Preheat the oven to 180°C/350°F/Gas 4.

Spread the wings out, with their marinade, in a large baking tin (pan) or dish and roast in the oven for 25 minutes, then spoon some of the marinade over the top, return to the oven and cook for a further 5–8 minutes, until sticky and glazed. (Alternatively, you can pan-fry the wings instead of baking.)

Serve with spring onions (scallions) and chilli scattered over.

VEGGIE FRIED RICE

(KHAO PAD PAK)

Serves 2

Cooking time: 20 minutes

2–3 tbsp vegetable oil

1 garlic clove, finely chopped

½ onion, finely chopped

150g (5oz) frozen mixed
  vegetables

220g (8oz) cooked cold jasmine
  rice

2 spring onions (scallions), finely
  sliced

2 eggs, whisked to combine

Salt and ground white pepper

For the sauce

1 tbsp soy sauce

1 tbsp vegan fish sauce

1 tbsp vegan oyster sauce

1 tsp sugar

Simply delicious vegan fried rice that can be made in 20 minutes, this is also very budget-friendly. I use mixed frozen veg as it's so handy and easy to get hold of, and also very cheap. Eat on its own or pair it up with a stir-fry or curry. You can replace the jasmine rice with wild rice, brown rice or even riceberry, if you can get hold of it, for a nuttier texture.

Heat the oil in a frying pan over a medium heat, add the garlic and fry for 1–2 minutes, until golden and crisp, then add the onion and frozen veg and cook for 2–3 minutes.

Add all the sauce ingredients, then stir to combine and coat the vegetables.

Add the cooked rice and mix well, using the back of a spatula to break down the rice and make sure all the grains are coated in sauce. Push the rice mixture to one side of the pan, add the eggs to the empty space, then mix them through the rice. Cook for 2–3 minutes, then take off the heat and sprinkle over the spring onions (scallions) and some salt and pepper to serve.

SPICY PAPAYA SALAD

(SOM TUM THAI)

A very popular Thai Isan dish that all Thai people fall in love with. The salad combines crunchy strips of unripe green papaya with garlic, chilli, green beans and a tangy dressing.

Serves 2

Cooking time: 15 minutes

¼ green papaya (you can also use kohlrabi or swede/rutabaga)

1 carrot

Handful of cashews or peanuts

1–2 garlic cloves, peeled

2 bird's eye chillies

1 tbsp palm sugar or brown sugar

Handful of green beans, cut into 4cm (1½in) lengths

Handful of cherry tomatoes, halved

2 tbsp fish sauce

Juice of 1 lime (2–3 tbsp)

½ tbsp tamarind paste

To serve
Baby gem lettuce or prawn crackers (optional)

Peel the papaya and carrot then cut them into narrow matchsticks (a julienne peeler is ideal, otherwise use a coarse grater).

Toast the cashews or peanuts in a dry pan for 5 minutes. Tip onto a plate and set aside.

Pound the garlic and chillies in a pestle and mortar until they form a rough paste. Add the sugar, green beans and tomatoes, lightly pound then mix it all together.

Add the papaya and carrot and mix with the pestle, pounding very lightly. Add the fish sauce, sugar, lime juice and tamarind paste and mix well. Add the toasted cashews or peanuts and lightly pound them all together. Toss to combine, tasting to make sure it is sweet, sour, salty and spicy, and adding more fish sauce or sugar if needed.

Serve with a side salad of baby gem, if you like, or with prawn crackers.

THAI FRIED RICE WITH CRAB

(KHAO PAD PUU)

Serves 2

Cooking time: 30 minutes

2 tbsp vegetable oil

2 garlic cloves, finely chopped

1 onion, finely sliced

½ carrot, finely diced

1 tbsp oyster sauce

1 tbsp soy sauce

2 tbsp fish sauce

1 tsp sugar

220g (8oz) cold cooked rice

1 or 2 eggs

200g (7oz) fresh or canned white crabmeat

Pinch each of salt and ground white pepper

To serve

2 spring onions (scallions), finely sliced

Ground white pepper

Lime wedges

Sliced cucumber

Nam pla prik (see page 175)

This is a very popular Thai street food dish you find at the seaside, and we often order it with other seafood dishes in place of regular steamed jasmine rice.

Heat the oil in a frying pan or wok over a medium heat. Add the garlic and stir for 1–2 minutes until golden. Add the onion and carrot and cook for a couple of minutes.

Add the oyster sauce, soy sauce, fish sauce and sugar, quickly mix until combined, then add the cooked rice. Cook for a few minutes, stirring to separate the grains and coat them evenly in the sauce.

Move the rice to one side of the pan and crack the egg(s) into the cleared space. Leave for a minute, then break the egg up with a spatula and start tossing the egg through the rice. Add the crabmeat, season with the salt and pepper and gently stir through the rice before removing from the heat.

Transfer to serving plates and top with spring onions (scallions) and some extra ground pepper if you like. Serve with a lime wedge, cucumber and nam pla prik.

Easy Swap
You can make this recipe with either fresh or canned crabmeat, or swap out the crabmeat for prawns (shrimp) or squid.

curry
IN A HURRY

THAI GREEN CHICKEN CURRY

(KAENG KIEW WAAN GAI)

Serves 2

Cooking time: 20 minutes

1 x 400g (14oz) can of coconut milk

1–2 tbsp Thai green curry paste (see page 178 for homemade)

250g (9oz) boneless, skinless chicken breast or thighs, cut into bite-sized pieces

1 carrot, chopped into chunks

½ large aubergine (eggplant) or 2–3 small Thai eggplants (about 220g/8oz), cut into 2.5cm (1in) pieces

2 handfuls of green beans

Handful of finely sliced (bell) peppers (ideally a mix of colours)

140g (5oz) drained bamboo shoots

1–2 tbsp fish sauce

½ tsp salt, or to taste

1–2 tbsp palm sugar or brown sugar

2–3 makrut lime leaves, central woody stem removed

2 red chillies, sliced

2–3 handfuls of Thai basil

To serve

Perfect jasmine rice (page 168)

This is the most popular Thai curry dish and the one that everyone knows. It's fresh, vibrant and spicy, and the colour from Thai green bird's eye chillies (the main ingredient in the curry paste) is so inviting. My version of Thai green curry includes readily available vegetables such as carrot, aubergine (eggplant) and (bell) pepper that you can simply grab from the supermarket.

Scoop 2–3 tablespoons of the thick part of the coconut milk into a saucepan and place over a high heat. When it starts bubbling, add the curry paste and stir for 1–2 minutes, until fragrant.

Add the chicken and carrot, then stir well and allow to cook for a couple of minutes. Then add the aubergine (eggplant), green beans, (bell) peppers and bamboo shoots. Season with the fish sauce, salt and sugar. Mix well and simmer until the vegetables are cooked through.

Tear the lime leaves into the curry, then add the remaining coconut milk, the chillies and basil. Stir to combine, then serve with jasmine rice.

Easy Swap

You can easily make this vegetarian. Simply replace the chicken with extra vegetables, leave out the fish sauce and omit the shrimp paste from the green curry paste, if using homemade (if using store-bought, simply select a vegetarian Thai green curry paste).

Substitute the makrut lime leaves with a little lemon or lime zest, if needed.

THAI RED PORK CURRY

(KAENG DEANG MUU)

Serves 2

Cooking time: 30 minutes

1 x 400g (14oz) can of coconut
   milk

1–2 tbsp Thai red curry paste (see
   page 179 for homemade)

250g (9oz) pork loin, finely sliced

3–4 baby aubergines (eggplants),
   cut into small bite-sized pieces

Handful of green beans, halved

1–2 tbsp brown sugar or palm
   sugar

2–3 tbsp fish sauce

2–3 makrut lime leaves, central
   woody stem removed, finely
   shredded, plus extra to finish

Handful of Thai basil leaves

1 red chilli, finely sliced

To serve
Perfect jasmine rice (page 168)

Thai red curry, widely eaten in Thailand, is warm and comforting, and perfect for a quick meal.

Scoop 2–3 tablespoons of the thick part of the coconut milk into a saucepan and place over a high heat. When it starts bubbling, add the curry paste and stir for 1–2 minutes, until fragrant.

Add the pork and cook for a few minutes, then add the aubergine (eggplant) and green beans, and stir well.

Season with the sugar, fish sauce and lime leaves, add about 125ml (4¼fl oz) more coconut milk and mix well, then simmer for 5–7 minutes.

Taste and adjust the saltiness, adding more fish sauce if preferred.

Stir in the basil, red chilli and extra shredded lime leaves before serving with steamed jasmine rice.

Easy Swap
This is also delicious using chicken or beef.

Substitute the makrut lime leaves with a little lemon or lime zest, if needed.

CHIANG MAI NOODLES

(KHAO SOI)

Serves: 2

Cooking time: 45 minutes

1 x 400g (14oz) can of coconut milk

2–3 tbsp khao soi curry paste (see page 182 for homemade)

4 chicken thighs, skinless but preferably bone-in

2–3 tbsp fish sauce

2–3 tbsp palm sugar or brown sugar

500ml (17fl oz) chicken stock or water

250g (9oz) egg noodles

Salt (optional)

For the deep-fried noodles
400–500ml (14–17fl oz) vegetable oil

250g (9oz) fresh egg noodles

For the toppings
Pickled mustard greens, rinsed well and finely chopped

Finely sliced shallots

Coriander (cilantro) leaves

Dried chilli flakes

To serve
Lime wedges

Thai chilli jam (nam prik pao)

This is a creamy coconut curry from the north region of Thailand, with tender chicken and a combination of chewy and crunchy noodles.

Scoop 3 tablespoons of the thick part of the coconut milk into a saucepan and place over a high heat. When it starts bubbling, add the curry paste. Mix well and when the oil begins to separate from the coconut milk and curry paste, add the chicken and the remaining coconut milk. Mix well and let it simmer for about 15 minutes.

Season with the fish sauce and sugar then add the chicken stock or water. Bring to the boil then reduce the heat to a low simmer. Cover and simmer until the chicken is cooked through and tender, about 30 minutes. Taste and season the curry with salt, fish sauce and more sugar if needed.

To deep-fry the noodles, pour the oil into a wok or small, deep saucepan (make sure it comes no more than two-thirds of the way up) and place over a medium heat. Have a plate lined with paper towels to hand. When the oil is hot, add a handful of egg noodles and deep-fry for 2–3 minutes until golden brown. Transfer to the lined plate and repeat to fry all the noodles. Set aside.

For the boiled noodles, cook in a pan of boiling water for 2 minutes then drain and divide between two bowls. Ladle the curry and chicken over the top of the boiled noodles, then add the deep-fried noodles and toppings. Serve with lime wedges and Thai sweet chilli sauce.

Easy Swap
You can also use chicken drumsticks, or beef or lamb.

In place of khao soi curry paste (if you can't find it and are not making your own), use 2 tablespoons of Thai red curry paste and add 1 teaspoon each of ground turmeric, ginger and cardamom.

PANANG BEEF CURRY

(KAENG PANANG NEU)

Serves 2

Cooking time: 30 minutes

½ x 400g (14oz) can of coconut milk

1–2 tbsp Panang curry paste (see page 178 for homemade)

1 rump (sirloin) steak, finely sliced

Handful of green beans, halved

1–2 tbsp brown sugar or palm sugar

2–3 tbsp fish sauce

1–2 makrut lime leaves, central woody stem removed, finely shredded

Handful of Thai basil leaves

To garnish
Finely sliced red chilli

1–2 makrut lime leaves, central woody stem removed, finely shredded

To serve
Perfect jasmine rice (page 168)

A rich, nutty Thai Panang curry goes so well with beef. While many Thai curries are quite brothy, Panang is more of a modest sauce that is rich, sweet, salty and nutty with a hint of spice from the cumin, coriander and nutmeg.

Scoop 2–3 tablespoons of the thick part of the coconut milk into a saucepan and place over over a high heat. When it starts bubbling, add the curry paste and stir-fry for 1–2 minutes, until fragrant.

Add the steak slices and cook for 3–4 minutes, then add the green beans and stir well.

Season with the sugar and fish sauce and add the lime leaves, then about 120ml (4fl oz/½ cup) coconut milk. Mix well and simmer for 5–7 minutes.

Taste and adjust the saltiness by adding more fish sauce if needed. Add the Thai basil leaves, give it a quick stir then remove from the heat.

Serve with steamed jasmine rice, garnished with the red chillies and lime leaves.

Easy Swap
You can find Panang curry paste online, in big supermarkets or a more authentic version in Asian grocery stores. For a 'cheat' version, you can simply use Thai red curry paste and mix it with 1 tablespoon of ground roasted peanuts before using.

I've used beef here, but do try using chicken, pork, prawns (shrimp) or tofu too.

Substitute the makrut lime leaves with a little lemon or lime zest, if needed.

CHOO CHEE CURRY WITH SALMON

(CHOO CHEE PLA SALMON)

Serves 2

Cooking time: 20 minutes

1 x 400g (14oz) can of coconut milk

1–2 tbsp Thai red curry paste (see page 179 for homemade)

2 salmon fillets (about 240g/8½oz in total)

2 tbsp palm sugar or brown sugar

1–1½ tbsp fish sauce (or 1–2 tbsp soy sauce)

1 tbsp roasted peanuts, ground in a pestle and mortar (optional; they make the sauce creamy and thick)

To garnish

1 red chilli, deseeded and finely sliced

2 makrut lime leaves, central woody stem removes, finely shredded

To serve

Perfect jasmine rice (page 168)

This is a great Thai home-style curry dish, and just like other typical Thai curries, it's so simple to make!

Scoop 2–3 tablespoons of the thick part of the coconut milk into a saucepan and place over a high heat. When it starts bubbling, add the curry paste and stir for 1–2 minutes, until fragrant.

Add the salmon fillets and cook for a few minutes, then flip them over and add 5–6 more tablespoons of coconut milk.

Add the sugar, fish sauce or soy sauce and simmer for about 5 minutes.

Taste and adjust the saltiness by adding more fish sauce, or soy sauce if preferred. Add a few more tablespoons of coconut milk and stir well. Add the ground peanuts, if using, and mix well.

To serve, transfer the curry to serving bowls, garnish with red chilli and shredded lime leaves and enjoy with steamed jasmine rice.

Easy Swap

This curry also works well with other seafood like king prawns (shrimp) or mackerel. To adapt to a vegan-friendly dish, use mixed veg or firm tofu instead of fish, use soy sauce instead of fish sauce, and omit the shrimp paste from the curry paste if using homemade (if using store-bought, select a vegan curry paste).

Substitute the makrut lime leaves with a little lemon or lime zest, if needed.

DUCK RED CURRY

(KAENG PED BPET YANG)

Red curry goes so well with duck – the rich flavour of the meat pairs surprisingly well with the rich, creamy coconut and spices.

Mix the five-spice sauce ingredients together in a dish. Using a very sharp knife, score the skin of the duck breasts in a criss-cross pattern, then add the breasts to the dish, coating them well. Leave to marinate for at least 15 minutes and up to 1 hour.

Preheat the oven to 200°C/400°F/Gas 6. Place an ovenproof frying pan over a medium heat and pan-fry the duck breasts (reserving the marinade) for 2–3 minutes on each side, then transfer to the oven (skin-side up) and roast for 20–30 minutes. Remove from the oven, rest on a board for 10 minutes, then slice.

Scoop 2–3 tablespoons of the thick part of the coconut milk into a saucepan and place over a high heat. When it starts bubbling, add the curry paste and stir for 1–2 minutes, until fragrant.

Next, add the duck slices and any juices from the roasting pan, along with the reserved marinade, and cook for a few minutes. Add the tomatoes and stir well. Season with the sugar, fish sauce and lime leaves. Add your chosen fruit, along with about 120ml (4fl oz/½ cup) coconut milk, then mix well and simmer for 5–7 minutes.

Taste and adjust the saltiness by adding more fish sauce if preferred. Add the Thai basil and stir for 1–2 minutes before removing from the heat. Serve garnished with the red chilli and lime leaves.

Easy Swap
Often tropical fruits like lychee and longan are added to this curry but, if you can't get hold of them, I have found English plums work really well.

Substitute the makrut lime leaves with a little lemon or lime zest, if needed.

Serves 2

Cooking time: 40 minutes, plus marinating

2 duck breasts

1 x 400g (14oz) can of coconut milk

1–2 tbsp Thai red curry paste (see page 179 for homemade)

Handful of cherry tomatoes

1–2 tbsp brown sugar or palm sugar

2–3 tbsp fish sauce

1–2 makrut lime leaves, central woody stem removed, finely shredded

Handful of fruit, such as lychees, longans or small plums, pitted and chopped into bite-sized pieces if necessary

Handful of Thai basil leaves

For the five-spice sauce

2 tbsp five-spice powder

2 tbsp oyster sauce

2 tbsp hoisin sauce

1 tsp dark sweet soy sauce (see page 14)

1 tsp honey

To garnish

Finely sliced red chilli

1–2 makrut lime leaves, central woody stem removed, finely shredded

MASSAMAN BEEF CURRY

(KAENG MASSAMAN NEU)

A rich, creamy, aromatic and mild curry introduced by Muslim traders from Persia, and which become very popular among Thai people.

Serves 2

Cooking time: 45 minutes

1 x 400g (14oz) can of coconut milk

2 tbsp massaman curry paste (see page 179 for homemade)

2 star anise

2 cinnamon sticks

300g (10½oz) stewing beef, cut into bite-sized pieces

1 small onion, chopped into large chunks

4–5 tbsp toasted peanuts (or cashews if you prefer)

1 medium potato, peeled and cut into chunks

3–4 tbsp fish sauce

2–3 tbsp palm sugar or brown sugar

1–2 tbsp tamarind paste

¼ red (bell) pepper, thickly sliced

½ large red chilli, finely sliced

To serve
Perfect jasmine rice (page 168)

Scoop 4–5 tablespoons of the thick part of the coconut milk into a saucepan and place over a high heat. When it starts bubbling, add the curry paste along with the star anise and cinnamon sticks and mix well. Cook until the red oil starts to separate and appear on the surface, then add the beef and stir well.

Next, add the onion, peanuts and potato, along with the remaining coconut milk. Mix to combine everything, then season with the fish sauce, sugar and tamarind paste. Give it a taste: it should be salty and sweet with a sourness cutting through the nutty flavour. Add the red (bell) pepper and chilli and mix well. Leave to cook for a further 30–45 minutes with a lid slightly open, or until the meat is tender.

Serve with jasmine rice.

Easy Swap
My mum would often add pineapple pieces to this massaman curry, which give a really nice flavour.

You can also swap the beef for bone-in chicken thighs or lamb shoulder.

If you can't find massaman curry paste and are not making your own, use 2 tablespoons of Thai red curry paste and add 1 teaspoon each of ground cloves, ground star anise and ground cinnamon.

CRAB CURRY

(KANOM JEEN NAM YA PUU)

Serves 2

Cooking time: 30 minutes

120g (4¼oz) cooked vermicelli rice noodles

4 tbsp vegetable oil

2 tbsp finely chopped garlic

1 x 400g (14oz) can of coconut milk

1–2 tbsp southern yellow curry paste (see below)

250g (9oz) cooked crabmeat (fresh or canned)

8–10 fish balls (optional)

1 tbsp fish sauce

1 tsp palm sugar or brown sugar

2–3 wild betel leaves, sliced (optional)

2–3 makrut lime leaves, central woody stems removed, torn

Handful of Thai basil leaves

For the southern yellow curry paste

Handful of Thai bird's eye chillies

2 shallots, finely sliced

2–4 garlic cloves, chopped

1 thumb-sized piece of galangal, finely sliced

2 lemongrass stalks (inside soft part only), finely sliced

1 tsp grated makrut lime zest (optional)

1 thumb-sized piece of fresh turmeric or 2 tsp ground turmeric

1 tbsp shrimp paste or miso paste

Pinch of salt

1 tbsp black peppercorns

To serve

Finely sliced red chilli

Fresh vegetables, such as green beans or cabbage

This delicious southern yellow curry-style dish of cooked crab is a must-have when I go to Thailand. It is typically served with fine rice noodles such as vermicelli, with lots of fresh vegetables on the side.

Pound all the curry paste ingredients together in a pestle and mortar until they form a paste.

Place the cooked vermicelli noodles in a large mixing bowl.

Add the oil to a small frying pan over a medium heat, then add the garlic and fry for 2–3 minutes until nice and golden. Add the garlic oil to the cooked noodles and toss. Set aside.

Scoop 3–4 tablespoons of the thick part of the coconut milk into a saucepan and place over a high heat. When it starts bubbling, add the curry paste and stir for 1–2 minutes, until fragrant.

Add about 1–2 tablespoons of crabmeat and all the fish balls (if using), then add the remaining coconut milk. Season with the fish sauce and sugar and stir well to mix.

Add the betel leaves (if using), the lime leaves and Thai basil. Mix well again and top with the remaining crabmeat.

Serve with the garlic noodles, sliced chilli and fresh vegetables.

Easy Swap

If you can't find crabmeat, try using fresh or canned mackerel and sardines instead. You'll find fish balls in the freezer section of Asian supermarkets.

For the paste, use standard lime zest instead of makrut and ginger in place of galangal, if needed.

JUNGLE CURRY

(KAENG PAA)

Serves 2

Cooking time: 30 minutes

1 tbsp Thai red curry paste (see page 179 for homemade)

1 lemongrass stalk, finely sliced

2–3 tbsp shredded lesser galangal (see page 10)

1 tbsp vegetable oil

500ml (17fl oz) vegetable stock or water

1 carrot, peeled and cut into bite-sized pieces

250g (9oz) pumpkin or butternut squash, peeled and cut into bite-sized pieces

50g (1¾oz) green beans, cut into bite-sized pieces

50g (1¾oz) baby corn, cut into bite-sized pieces

80g (3oz) mixed mushrooms

2–3 vines of fresh baby green peppercorns (use brined if you can't find fresh)

1 tbsp fish sauce

1 tsp sugar

1 tbsp toasted ground rice (see page 169)

Handful of Thai basil leaves

Another classic, tasty Thai recipe that is also vegetarian, this dish is from the mountain city of Chiang Mai. It is originally made with ingredients found in the jungles of Thailand (hence its name) and is a water-based curry without coconut milk (because you can't find coconuts in the jungle!).

Put the curry paste, lemongrass and 1 tablespoon of the lesser galangal in a pestle and mortar and pound until it becomes a paste.

Heat the oil in a saucepan over a medium heat and add the paste. Fry for 2–3 minutes then add the stock or water and bring to the boil.

Add all the vegetables and simmer for about 10 minutes, until tender and cooked, then add the peppercorns and season with the fish sauce and sugar. Add the toasted ground rice and mix well again.

Stir in the remaining lesser galangal and the Thai basil, allow to simmer for a further 2–3 minutes, then serve.

Easy Swap
If you can't find lesser galangal use fresh ginger instead.

To make this vegetarian/vegan, leave out the fish sauce and use miso paste instead of shrimp paste in your curry paste if making homemade (if using store-bought, purchase a vegan curry paste).

RUN JUAN CURRY

(KAENG RUN JUAN)

Serves 4

Cooking time: 45 minutes

500–750ml (17–25fl oz) vegetable stock

3–4 tbsp nam prik ka pi (see page 127)

3–4 baby shallots, halved and bashed

2 lemongrass stalks, chopped and bashed

1–2 garlic cloves, peeled and bashed

2–3 small bird's eye chillies

250g (9oz) boneless, skinless chicken thighs or pork loin, cut into long strips

1 tbsp palm sugar or brown sugar

1 tbsp fish sauce

Handful of Thai basil leaves

Juice of 1 lime (2–3 tbsp)

To serve

Perfect jasmine rice (page 168)

This is an old royal Thai curry that you don't often see in Thailand anymore, let alone outside Thailand. It's the perfect way to use up the leftover nam prik ka pi on page 127. It's so simple yet so tasty.

Add the stock to a saucepan over a medium heat. Add the nam prik ka pi, mix well then add the shallots, lemongrass, garlic and chillies. Boil for about 2–3 minutes.

Add the chicken or pork, turn the heat down, gently stir and simmer for 10–12 minutes.

Season with the sugar and fish sauce, add the Thai basil, then take off the heat and squeeze in the lime juice. Serve with jasmine rice.

THAI YELLOW LAMB CURRY

(KAENG KARI KEA)

Serves 4

Cooking time: 50 minutes

1 x 400g (14oz) can of coconut milk

2 tbsp yellow curry paste (see page 179 for homemade)

250g (9oz) diced stewing lamb (shoulder is best)

1 onion, chopped in big chunks

1 medium potato, peeled and cut into chunks

2–3 tbsp fish sauce

2–3 tbsp palm sugar or brown sugar

1 large red chilli, finely sliced

To serve
Perfect jasmine rice (page 168), naan bread or roti (optional)

Thai curries are not often made with lamb, but due to the Indian roots of Thai yellow curry paste I find it is the perfect combination here – delicious, mild and fragrant.

Scoop 3–4 tablespoons of the thick part of the coconut milk into a saucepan and place over a high heat. When it starts bubbling, add the curry paste and stir for 1–2 minutes, until fragrant.

Add the diced lamb and stir for 2–3 minutes before adding the remaining coconut milk, mixing well.

Stir in the onion and potato and season with the fish sauce and sugar. Give it a taste: it should be salty, sweet and nutty. Add more fish sauce or sugar if needed.

Stir in the chilli and leave to cook over a low heat for a further 35–45 minutes or until the meat is tender. Add a little bit of water if it seems to be getting too dry – you want the sauce to be quite wet. Serve with steamed jasmine rice, naan bread or roti.

Easy Swap
This curry is lovely with chicken or beef too, so use what you have available.

my mum's
KITCHEN

STIR-FRIED ASPARAGUS WITH PRAWNS IN OYSTER SAUCE

(PAD NOR MAI FARANG KUUNG)

Serves 2

Cooking time: 15 minutes

2 tbsp vegetable oil

1 garlic clove, finely chopped

180g (6oz) raw peeled prawns (shrimp)

12 asparagus spears, woody ends trimmed

1 tbsp fish sauce

1 tbsp soy sauce

1 tsp sugar

Ground black pepper

To serve
Perfect jasmine rice (page 168)

An easy, quick and balanced stir-fry, perfect for a midweek meal after a long day at work.

Heat the oil in a frying pan or wok over a medium heat, add the garlic and cook, stirring, for 1–2 minutes until it turns golden and crisp.

Add the prawns (shrimp) and cook for 5 minutes, tossing them occasionally. Next, add the asparagus, stir well and cook for a further 5–6 minutes.

Season with the fish sauce, soy sauce, sugar and ground pepper. Toss everything together then serve with jasmine rice.

Easy Swap
You can replace the asparagus with green beans or broccoli, if you prefer.

PORK AND CHILLI DIP

(NAM PHRIK ONG)

Serves 3–4 as a sharing platter

Cooking time: 20 minutes

1 tsp vegetable oil

2 garlic cloves, finely chopped

150g (5oz) minced (ground) pork

1 onion, finely chopped

1 tbsp Thai red curry paste (see page 179 for homemade)

6–8 tomatoes, finely chopped

Pinch of salt

2 tbsp tamarind paste

2 tbsp palm sugar or brown sugar

1 tbsp fish sauce

Handful of coriander (cilantro), roughly chopped

To serve

Selection of crunchy raw vegetables, for dipping

Thai sticky rice (see page 168)

This dish of chilli paste with minced (ground) pork is originally from northern Thailand but is very popular among Thai people. Place in the centre of the table for everyone to share as a snack.

Heat the oil in a saucepan over a medium heat, add the garlic and fry for 1–2 minutes, until fragrant. Add the chicken or pork and stir well, breaking down the clumps, until it is nearly all cooked.

Add the onion and cook for about 5 minutes until soft, then stir in the curry paste. Add the tomatoes and mix well.

Add the salt, and a little water if the mixture seems too thick, then stir in the tamarind paste and sugar until combined.

Let it simmer for about 5–8 minutes, then mix through the fish sauce. By now the consistency should be dippable. Taste: it should be sweet and sour, then salty and spicy to follow.

Spread in a shallow bowl, then sprinkle over the coriander (cilantro) and serve with your choice of fresh vegetables and sticky rice, if you like.

Easy Swap

You can use chicken in place of the pork.

Nam phrik ong is essentially a dip, and is commonly served with sticky rice, pork crackling and fresh crunchy vegetables such as cucumber, green beans, Chinese cabbage and lettuce. Use whatever crunchy vegetables you have to hand that can be used for scooping.

'CAT RICE'

(KHAO MAEW)

Serves 2

Cooking time: 15 minutes

1 tbsp vegetable oil

2 fillets of sea bass

220g (8oz) cold cooked rice

1–2 tbsp fish sauce or soy sauce

2 shallots, finely sliced

1–2 garlic cloves, finely sliced

Bunch of dill, finely chopped

Bunch of chives, finely chopped

½ cucumber, sliced

5–8 green beans, finely chopped

Handful of grated carrot

1 spring onion (scallion), finely
   chopped

1 lime, cut into wedges

Salt and ground white pepper

To garnish

1–2 tbsp finely chopped chilli

Coriander (cilantro)

This is, simply, spicy fried fish mixed with rice and vegetables, but because Thai cats love fish (don't all cats?!), we call this dish 'cat rice' – *khao* meaning 'rice' and *maew* 'cat'. This recipe always reminds me of my childhood – I would always ask my mum to make it when we had leftover rice.

Preheat the grill (broiler) to medium and line a baking tray with baking parchment.

Rub the oil over both sides of the sea bass fillets and place on the lined baking tray, skin side up. Grill (broil) for 10–12 minutes, until cooked through and the skin is lightly crisp. (You can pan-fry the fillets if you prefer.) Transfer to a plate to cool a little, before breaking one fillet into small pieces and the other fillet into larger pieces. Set aside.

Place the cooked rice in a frying pan over a low heat, add the smaller fish pieces and stir well for 1 minute. Season with the fish sauce or soy sauce, salt and pepper, give it a quick stir and take off the heat.

Spoon the rice into the middle of 2 serving plates and arrange the herbs and vegetables nicely around the rice. Add the larger pieces of sea bass next to the vegetables, then garnish with the chilli and coriander (cilantro).

Squeeze over some lime juice before mixing everything together and enjoying.

Easy Swap

You can replace the fish with ready-cooked smoked mackerel, and skip the first step.

SON-IN-LAW EGGS

(KAI LOUG KHEUH)

Serves 2

Cooking time: 20 minutes

4 baby shallots, finely sliced
  lengthwise

120ml (4fl oz/½ cup) vegetable oil,
  plus extra for deep-frying

4 eggs, boiled for 8-10 minutes
  then peeled (I use duck eggs as
  they have a rich yolk – if using
  hen eggs, boil for 7-9 minutes)

Sliced red chilli and coriander
  (cilantro) leaves, to garnish

For the sauce

60g (2oz) palm sugar or brown
  sugar

2 tbsp fish sauce

2 tbsp tamarind paste

About 4 tbsp water

To serve

Perfect jasmine rice (page 168),
  optional

Fried boiled eggs in tamarind sauce is a favourite dish among kids – just about every Thai mum has made this for her kids, as it has all the Thai sweet and sour flavours and goes well with rice and other Thai dishes. There are many stories behind the name, but the best known is about a mother who thinks that her daughter isn't being treated well by her son-in-law, so serves him deep-fried eggs to let him know that he needs to treat her daughter better, or else! Another (nicer) story stems from the fact that eggs are a staple ingredient in Thailand, so mothers cook this dish often and it has therefore become a favourite of sons-in-law everywhere.

Add the sliced shallots and oil to a small pan over a medium heat. Stirring constantly, cook for 3–4 minutes until golden brown and crisp. Using a slotted spoon, transfer the fried shallots to a plate lined with paper towels; set aside.

Discard the oil and add the sauce ingredients. Bring to a gentle boil, stirring constantly. Once the sugar has fully dissolved, check the sauce's consistency, which should be that of maple syrup; continue cooking over a low heat until it reaches that consistency, if necessary.

Meanwhile, add enough oil for deep-frying to a medium, heavy-based pan or wok, making sure it is no more than half-full. Place over a medium-high heat and, once the oil is hot, gently drop the peeled boiled eggs into it. Gently move them around to ensure even browning, and, once the surface is thoroughly browned, lift them out with a slotted spoon, slice them in half and arrange on a serving platter.

Pour the sauce over the eggs. Sprinkle the fried shallots over the top of the eggs, then garnish with the chilli and coriander (cilantro) Eat as a snack or serve with steamed jasmine rice.

Easy Swap
If you don't want to go to the effort of boiling then frying your eggs, simply fry the eggs as you usually would, then spoon over the sauce and toppings. Made like this, the dish is called daughter-in-law eggs.

SWEET AND SOUR VEG WITH CHICKEN
(GAI PAD PEAW WAAN)

Serves 2

Cooking time: 20 minutes

1 tbsp vegetable oil

1 tbsp finely chopped garlic

200g (7oz) boneless, skinless chicken breast or thighs, cut into bite-sized pieces

1 onion, chopped

1 red (bell) pepper, chopped

50g (1¾oz) baby corn, halved diagonally

Handful of broccoli florets, cut into bite-sized pieces

150g (5oz) diced fresh pineapple

40g (1½oz) toasted cashews

For the sweet and sour sauce

2 tbsp Thai sweet chilli sauce (see page 172 for homemade)

1 tbsp oyster sauce

1 tbsp tomato ketchup

1 tbsp soy sauce

1 tbsp maple syrup

1 tbsp cornflour (cornstarch)

Pinch each of salt and ground black pepper

To serve

Steamed rice

Sweet, sour, salty and sticky, this is so comfortingly moreish!

Mix the sweet and sour sauce ingredients together in a bowl and set aside.

Heat the oil in a frying pan or wok over a medium heat, add the garlic and fry for 1–2 minutes until golden and crisp. Add the chicken and fry for 2–3 minutes.

Add all the vegetables and pineapple, give everything a quick stir and cook, stirring, for 6–8 minutes.

Turn the heat to low, add the sweet and sour sauce and stir briefly until the sauce thickens, adding a splash of water if it seems too thick. Stir through the cashews and serve with rice.

Easy Swap
Feel free to use canned pineapple instead of fresh.

MY GRANDMA'S STICKY PORK BELLY

(KAI PALOW KHUN YAY)

Serves 4

Cooking time: 60 minutes

2–3 tbsp vegetable oil

1kg (2lb 3oz) pork belly (side), cut into 2–3cm (¾–1¼in) cubes

4 baby shallots, finely sliced

6–8 garlic cloves, finely chopped

10g (½oz) ginger, grated, plus 25g (1oz), finely sliced

1 tbsp dark sweet soy sauce (see page 14)

3 tbsp light soy sauce

3 tsp brown sugar

2 star anise

2 cinnamon sticks

3 tbsp oyster sauce

3 tsp honey

3 long red chillies, sliced

1 litre (34fl oz/4¼ cups) stock or water

2 carrots, chopped in chunks

Bunch of Thai basil, leaves only

To serve

2 hard-boiled eggs

Steamed rice

This delicious Chinese-style braise is a childhood favourite of mine that brings me happy memories every time I cook it.

Heat the oil in a wok or large saucepan over a medium-high heat. Add the pork, shallots, garlic, grated ginger and half of the sliced ginger.

Fry until the pork belly is lightly caramelized then turn the heat down to medium. Add the soy sauces, sugar, star anise, cinnamon, oyster sauce, honey and two-thirds of the chillies. Combine well.

Add the stock or water and bring to the boil. Add the carrots and reduce to a simmer for 50–60 minutes until the liquid has reduced.

Take off the heat, mix in the basil leaves and remaining chilli slices and sliced ginger, then serve with the hard-boiled eggs and some steamed rice.

Easy Swap

Try making this with pork or beef ribs in place of the pork belly.

THAI CRISPY OMELETTE

(KAI JEOW)

Serves 1

Cooking time: 10 minutes

2 eggs

1 tbsp fish sauce

2 spring onions (scallions), finely chopped

Squeeze of juice from a wedge of lime (about 1 tsp)

Pinch of ground white pepper

Handful of Thai basil (optional)

100ml (3½fl oz) vegetable oil

To serve

Sriracha sauce or nam pla prik (see page 175)

This is a very popular, staple dish that we often have in Thailand. You can have it for breakfast, serve it with rice or pair it with some sticky dishes such as curry or spicy salad. The special feature of a Thai omelette is that it is crispy around the outside but soft in the middle. It's absolutely delicious.

Add the eggs, fish sauce, spring onions (scallions), lime juice, pepper and Thai basil, if using, to a mixing bowl. Use a fork to whisk until combined and frothy.

Heat the oil in a wok or frying pan over a high heat. Once hot, pour in the egg mixture and let it cook until nice and fluffy, then turn over and let the other side cook, until the edges are crispy.

Transfer to a plate and serve with Sriracha or nam pla prik.

Easy Swap
You can add minced (ground) pork, chicken or prawns, if you like – simply add the raw meat to the egg mixture before cooking.

STIR-FRIED CHICKEN AND GINGER

(GAI PAD KING)

Serves 2

Cooking time: 15 minutes

1–2 tbsp vegetable oil

1 garlic clove, finely chopped

150g (5oz) boneless, skinless chicken thighs or breast, cut into bite-sized pieces

1 small onion, finely sliced

1 tbsp oyster sauce

1–2 tbsp soy sauce

1 tsp sugar

¼ red (bell) pepper, sliced

2 spring onions (scallions), finely shredded

1 thumbnail-sized piece of ginger, finely sliced

½ large red chilli, finely sliced

Ground black pepper

To serve
Noodles or steamed rice

Simply delicious chicken with ginger and oyster sauce, this is perfect for a quick and easy midweek meal. This is my nan's favourite dish to cook for me, especially when I feel under the weather. She says the ginger will make me feel better!

Heat the oil in a work or frying pan over a medium heat. Add the garlic and fry for 1–2 minutes until golden, then add the chicken and stir-fry for 2–3 minutes.

Add the onion and stir well for 2 minutes, then season with the oyster sauce, soy sauce and sugar and give everything a good toss together.

Add the (bell) pepper, spring onions (scallions), ginger and chilli. Stir-fry over a medium-high heat for 1–2 minutes, or until the chicken is cooked through.

Add a splash of water to loosen up the sauce a little, stir to combine, then sprinkle with black pepper and serve with rice or noodles.

Easy Swap
You can substitute prawns (shrimp), fish or tofu for the chicken, or even pork or beef.

BEEF AND BROCCOLI IN OYSTER SAUCE

(NUE PAD NAM MUN HOI)

Serves 2

Cooking time: 15 minutes

1–2 tbsp vegetable oil

2 garlic cloves, finely chopped

200g (7oz) rump (sirloin) steak, finely sliced

½ onion, sliced

Handful of broccoli, cut into bite-sized pieces

Couple of handfuls of finely sliced mixed colour (bell) peppers

2 tbsp oyster sauce

1 tbsp fish sauce

1 tsp sugar

Pinch each of salt and ground white pepper

To serve

Noodles or steamed rice

A simply delicious one-pan dish that you can prepare in under 15 minutes! The tasty beef is flavoured with umami oyster sauce and served with a bowl of plain rice to create a perfect fakeaway dinner. It is very savoury and quite addictive.

Heat the oil in a frying pan or wok over a medium heat. Add the garlic and stir for 1–2 minutes until it turns golden and crisp.

Add the beef and onion, stir-fry for 5 minutes, then add the broccoli and (bell) peppers and cook for 5 minutes more.

Season with the oyster sauce, fish sauce, sugar, salt and pepper. Give it a quick stir then serve with noodles or rice.

Easy Swap

This works well with pork, prawns (shrimp) or mushrooms in place of the beef.

MEATBALL CONGEE

(KAO TOM)

My most favourite Thai breakfast ever! Delicious and so comforting – you must give this a go. Next time you're cooking rice, make a little extra and use the leftovers for this dish the following day.

Serves 2

Cooking time: 25 minutes

450ml (15fl oz) water

1 chicken or vegetable stock cube

220g (8oz) cold cooked rice

2 spring onions (scallions), finely sliced

2 tbsp fish sauce

1 tbsp soy sauce

1 tsp ground white pepper

For the pork or chicken balls

200g (7oz) minced (ground) pork or chicken

1 tbsp fish sauce

1 tsp grated garlic

1 tbsp soy sauce

Pinch of ground white pepper

For the crispy garlic

3 tbsp vegetable oil

3–4 garlic cloves, finely chopped

To garnish

A few coriander (cilantro) stalks, roughly chopped, plus a few whole leaves

½ large red chilli, thinly sliced (optional)

Ground white pepper (optional)

Combine the water and stock cube in a saucepan and bring to the boil. Once the stock is boiling, add the cooked rice, reduce to a simmer, partially cover with a lid and cook for 8–10 minutes, stirring occasionally.

Meanwhile, combine the pork or chicken ball ingredients in a bowl, then form the mixture into small balls, about 2–3cm (¾–1¼in) in diameter.

Remove the lid from the rice and add the meatballs to the pan. Cook for 5 minutes, stirring occasionally, then add half the spring onions (scallions), and a little more water if it looks like it is drying out. Gently stir for a couple more minutes.

For the crispy garlic, heat the oil in a small saucepan over a medium heat, add the garlic and fry, stirring, for 2–3 minutes until crispy and golden. Tip into a small bowl.

Season the rice congee with the fish sauce and soy sauce, adding more to taste if needed.

Spoon the congee into bowls and top with the crispy garlic and oil and remaining spring onions, season with white pepper, and garnish with coriander (cilantro) and chilli.

Easy Swap

Fresh king prawns (shrimp), squid or salmon are also very nice in place of the pork or chicken.

STIR-FRIED SQUASH WITH EGG

(PAD FAK TONG)

Serves 2

Cooking time: 20 minutes

2 tbsp vegetable oil

2 garlic cloves, finely chopped

280g (10oz) butternut squash
   or pumpkin, peeled, deseeded
   and cut into small chunks
   (2.5cm/1in)

1 tbsp fish sauce

2 tbsp soy sauce

1 tbsp oyster sauce

1 tbsp sugar

2 eggs

A little finely sliced red chilli

Handful of Thai basil leaves

Salt and ground white pepper

To serve
Perfect jasmine rice (page 168)

This is a super-nutritious and tasty, quick stir-fry, perfect for a midweek supper.

Heat the oil in a frying pan or wok over a medium-high heat, add the garlic and fry for 1–2 minutes until golden. Add the squash and stir-fry for 10 minutes until tender.

Add the fish sauce, soy sauce, oyster sauce and sugar, then stir to coat the pumpkin.

Add the eggs and leave to half-cook before mixing them through the other ingredients.

Season with salt and pepper, add the chilli and Thai basil, give it all a quick toss, then serve with jasmine rice.

PAN-FRIED SALMON

(SALMON TORD NAM PLA)

Serves: 2

Cooking time: 20 minutes

2 tbsp fish sauce

1 tsp each of salt and ground black pepper

2 salmon fillets (about 240g/8½oz in total)

2 tbsp plain (all-purpose) flour

3 tbsp vegetable oil

Coriander (cilantro), to garnish (optional)

For the salsa

¼ raw sour mango or Granny Smith apple, finely sliced into matchsticks/julienne

1 tbsp sugar

Juice of 1 lime (2–3 tbsp)

2 tbsp fish sauce

2 bird's eye chillies, finely sliced

1 shallot, finely sliced

A light and healthy salmon dish with tasty Thai-style salsa, this pairs well with some steamed vegetables.

Massage the fish sauce, salt and pepper into the salmon fillets, then sprinkle the flour on both sides. Transfer to a plate lined with paper towels and set aside.

Heat the oil in a frying pan set over a medium heat, add the salmon and fry for about 3 minutes on each side, until just cooked through. Alternatively, wrap in foil, place on a baking tray and bake for 20 minutes in a 180°C/350°F/Gas 4 oven.

For the salsa, mix all the ingredients together well. Taste and add more lime juice or fish sauce if needed.

Serve the salmon alongside the salsa and scatter with coriander (cilantro), if you like.

Easy Swap
This is also lovely with sea bass.

CARROT TOP OMELETTE WITH CHILLI DIP

(NAM PRIK KA PI CHA OM TORD)

Serves 2 as a sharing dish

Cooking time: 35 minutes

3 eggs

1 tbsp fish sauce

Pinch of ground white pepper

2 handfuls of green carrot tops, washed and finely chopped

100ml (3½fl oz) vegetable oil

For the nam prik ka pi

2 garlic cloves, peeled

2–3 bird's eye chillies

3 baby shallots, chopped

1 tbsp dried shrimp

1 tbsp palm sugar or brown sugar

1 tbsp shrimp paste

Juice of 1 lime (2–3 tbsp)

1 tsp fish sauce (optional; if needed)

Nam prik ka pi is a traditional Thai dipping paste that we usually serve with Thai mackerel, lots of vegetables and Thai-style omelette for dipping.

For the nam prik ka pi, pound the garlic, chillies, shallots and dried shrimp together in a pestle and mortar. Once it forms a fine paste, add the sugar and shrimp paste and pound until it all combines.

Add the lime juice and fish sauce (taste the paste first: if it's very salty already there's no need to add the fish sauce), then mix well and transfer to a small serving bowl.

For the omelette, add the eggs, fish sauce, pepper and carrot tops to a mixing bowl. Use a fork to whisk until combined and frothy.

Heat the oil in a frying pan over a medium heat and add the beaten eggs. Cook until nice and fluffy, then turn over and let the other side cook until the edges are crispy. Remove from the pan and cut into small bite-sized squares, then serve with the nam prik ka pi.

Easy Swap

This Thai-style omelette is usually made with a vegetable called acacia or cha-om, but I use carrot tops instead, as they are much easier to find outside Thailand.

STIR-FRIED CHICKEN WITH CRISPY GARLIC

(GAI KRA TIEM)

Serves 2

Cooking time: 15 minutes

3 tbsp vegetable oil

4 garlic cloves, finely chopped

250g (9oz) boneless, skinless chicken breast or thighs, cut into thin strips (2 x 4.5cm/¾ x 1¾in)

2 tbsp finely chopped spring onion (scallion)

For the sauce

2 tbsp oyster sauce

1 tbsp fish sauce

1 tbsp soy sauce

1 tbsp brown sugar

1 tsp ground white pepper

To serve

Sriracha sauce (optional)

Perfect jasmine rice (page 168)

This is my all-time favourite dish that my mum cooked for me when I was young. Now I cook this for my family and it has become their all-time favourite too!

Heat the oil in a wok or pan over a medium-high heat, add the garlic and stir well for 1–2 minutes until it turns crispy and golden. Using a slotted spoon, transfer to a small plate and set aside.

Add the chicken to the wok and stir-fry for 6–7 minutes.

Add all the sauce ingredients and stir for 2–3 minutes, adding 2–3 tablespoons of water if the sauce seems too dry.

Top with spring onion (scallion) and crispy garlic and serve with jasmine rice. Drizzle with Sriracha for extra spice, if you like.

STEAMED COD WITH GINGER AND SOY

(PLA NUENG SEE EW)

Serves 2

Cooking time: 25 minutes

2 cod fillets

2 tsp soy sauce

1 tsp sesame oil

1 thumb-sized piece of ginger, finely sliced into matchsticks

½ small onion, finely sliced

1–2 red chillies, finely sliced

Coriander (cilantro) leaves, to garnish

For the dipping sauce

1 tbsp miso paste

1 tsp grated ginger

1 tsp grated garlic

2 tbsp lime juice

1 tsp soy sauce

Steaming is a common cooking method in Thai cuisine, and one that retains the moisture within the food. This is a delicious version of a steamed fish recipe handed down to me from my dad.

Mix all the ingredients for the dipping sauce together in a small bowl and set aside.

Cut out a piece of baking parchment big enough to generously wrap both fish fillets. Place the fillets in the centre of the parchment then top with the soy sauce, sesame oil, ginger, onion and chilli.

Loosely wrap the parchment over the fish into a parcel, securing it with kitchen string.

Using a vegetable or bamboo steamer, steam the parcel for 10–12 minutes over a medium heat.

Carefully open up the parcel and transfer the fish to plates. Garnish with coriander (cilantro) and serve alongside seasonal vegetables and the dipping sauce.

Easy Swap
Substitute the cod with any white fish such as hake, pollock or haddock.

plant-based
THAI

STIR-FRIED TOFU
(PAD TAO HUU PRIK GAENG)

Serves 4

Cooking time: 20 minutes

1 block (about 390g/14oz) firm tofu, cut into 2.5cm (1in) wide strips (you can also use paneer)

2 tbsp plain (all-purpose) flour, seasoned with a pinch each of salt and pepper

200ml (7fl oz) vegetable oil, plus 1 tbsp

2 tbsp vegan Thai red curry paste (see page 179 for homemade)

Handful of green beans, halved

1 tbsp vegan fish sauce or soy sauce

1 tbsp palm sugar or brown sugar

Handful of Thai basil leaves

3–4 makrut lime leaves, central woody stem removed, thinly sliced

1 large red chilli, finely sliced, to garnish

To serve
Perfect jasmine rice (page 168), optional

This is a dish that I enjoy eating when I don't fancy having meat. Shallow-frying the tofu makes it lovely and crispy before it is cooked in the tasty curry.

Pat the tofu with paper towels to get rid of excess water, then coat in the seasoned flour.

Heat the 200ml (7fl oz) oil in a frying pan or wok over a medium heat, add the tofu and shallow-fry for 10–12 minutes or until the outside is nicely crisp and golden. Remove with a slotted spoon and place on paper towels to drain.

Remove the vegetable oil from the pan and add the tablespoon of fresh oil. Place over a medium heat and add the curry paste. Cook for 2–3 minutes, stirring constantly.

Add the green beans, toss and cook for 2–3 minutes. Season with the vegan fish or soy sauce and the sugar, then mix well.

Add the fried tofu back to the pan and stir well to coat it evenly in the sauce (at this point you can add a splash of water if the sauce becomes too dry).

Add the basil leaves, lime leaves and chilli, toss together and serve with jasmine rice or just as it is.

Easy Swap
Try green, yellow or jungle curry paste instead of red for a different type of heat.

If you can't get hold of makrut lime leaves, use the zest of a lemon or lime instead.

VEGAN THAI GREEN CURRY

(KAENG KIEW WAAN JAY)

Serves 4

Cooking time: 25 minutes

1 x 400g (14oz) can of coconut milk

2 tbsp vegan Thai green curry paste (see page 178 for homemade)

1 aubergine (eggplant), chopped into bite-sized pieces

1 carrot, chopped into bite-sized pieces

1 courgette (zucchini), chopped into bite-sized pieces

¼ cauliflower, chopped into bite-sized pieces

70g (2½oz) green beans, halved

¼ cabbage, chopped into bite-sized pieces

225g (8oz) canned bamboo shoots, drained

2–3 vegan fish sauce or soy sauce

1 tbsp palm sugar or brown sugar

3–4 makrut lime leaves, central woody stem removed, torn in half

Handful of Thai basil leaves

To serve
Perfect jasmine rice (page 168)

A rich and delicious one-pot plant-based Thai green curry that is packed full of vegetables and flavour.

Scoop 2 tablespoons of the thick part of the coconut milk into a saucepan and place over a high heat. When it starts bubbling, add the curry paste and stir for 1–2 minutes, until fragrant.

Add another 3 tablespoons of coconut milk and stir well, then reduce the heat to a simmer. Add the aubergine (eggplant) and carrot and cook for a few minutes, before adding the courgette (zucchini), cauliflower, green beans and cabbage. Stir and cook for a further 12–15 minutes.

Add the remaining coconut milk and mix well, then add the bamboo shoots and cook for 2–3 minutes. Season with the vegan fish sauce or soy sauce and sugar, and add a little water if the sauce is too thick.

Remove from the heat, stir through the lime leaves and basil leaves and serve with jasmine rice.

Easy Swap
You can adapt this to use any seasonal ingredients you have to hand – why not try Brussels sprouts in winter?

If you can't get hold of makrut lime leaves, use the zest of a lemon or lime instead.

CRISPY CAULIFLOWER IN SWEET TAMARIND SAUCE

(DOK KA LUM KROB SAUCE MAKAM)

Serves 2

Cooking time: 30 minutes

130g (4½oz) self-raising flour

2 tbsp panko breadcrumbs

Pinch each of salt and ground white pepper

180ml (6fl oz) cold sparkling water

½ cauliflower, cut into bite-sized pieces

470ml (16fl oz/2 cups) vegetable oil

For the sweet tamarind sauce

1 tbsp tamarind paste

4 tbsp palm sugar or brown sugar

1 tbsp vegan fish sauce or soy sauce

4–5 tbsp water

To garnish

1–2 dried chillies

Handful of Thai basil

Crispy fried shallots (optional; see page 110)

The combination of tamarind paste, palm sugar and vegan fish sauce gives this crispy cauliflower the perfect balance of sweet, salty and sour flavours that Thai cuisine is known for. The cauliflower here replaces the traditional chicken balls, but trust me, you wouldn't know as it's so tasty and elevates the cauliflower to new heights. Plus, it's super-easy to make!

For the sweet tamarind sauce, combine all the ingredients in a small pan over a medium-high heat. Keep stirring until the sugar dissolves and the sauce thickens, then remove from the heat.

Mix the flour, panko breadcrumbs, salt and pepper in a mixing bowl, then add the sparkling water and mix until you have a thick batter. If the batter doesn't seem loose enough to coat the cauliflower, add a little more water, a tablespoonful at a time. Add the cauliflower to the batter and mix well until all the pieces are coated.

Heat the oil in a deep frying pan, wok or saucepan over a medium heat. When hot, add the cauliflower pieces in batches, a few at a time, and fry until golden and crisp. Remove with a slotted spoon and place on a plate lined with paper towels to absorb excess oil.

Add the dried chillies and basil to the same pan and fry in the hot oil for a few minutes or until they start to crisp up. Remove with a slotted spoon.

To serve, place the crispy cauliflower in a large mixing bowl and add the sweet tamarind sauce. Toss the cauliflower and sauce together, then transfer to a serving dish. Top with the crispy fried chilli and basil, and crispy fried shallots, if using.

MUSHROOM TOM YUM WITH RICE NOODLES

(KEOW TEOW TOMYUM JAY)

Serves 2

Cooking time: 25 minutes

120g (4¼oz) vermicelli rice noodles

1–2 tbsp vegetable oil

600ml (20fl oz/2½ cups) vegetable stock or water

2 lemongrass stalks, bashed, green part removed and chopped into 3cm (1¼in slices)

2 large red chillies, finely sliced

2–3 tbsp soy sauce

1 tsp sugar

2 tbsp chilli jam or chilli oil (optional)

200g (7oz) closed cup mushrooms (or another type of mushroom), thinly sliced

3 makrut lime leaves, central woody stem removed, torn

100g (3½oz) beansprouts

Handful of coriander (cilantro), roughly chopped

Juice of 2 limes (3–4 tbsp)

5–6 Thai basil leaves

1 tbsp dried chilli flakes, for extra heat (optional)

This is an easy sweet-and-sour dish bursting with flavour. Traditionally made with seafood, it works so well with mushrooms too and has all the authentic flavours and spice from the Thai herbs.

To cook the rice noodles, bring a medium pan of water to the boil, add the noodles and cook for 2 minutes. Drain, divide between two bowls, add the oil and mix well to stop the noodles sticking together.

Add the stock or water to the same pan and bring to the boil. Add the lemongrass, chillies, soy sauce, sugar and chilli jam or oil, if using (for extra heat and colour). Mix well and cook for 2–3 minutes.

Add the mushrooms and cook for 5 minutes, then add the lime leaves, beansprouts, most of the coriander (cilantro) and the lime juice. Stir well for 2 minutes, then taste and adjust the flavour, adding more soy or lime juice as you prefer.

Take off the heat and pour evenly over the noodles. Top each bowl with some Thai basil, reserved coriander and the chilli flakes, if using. Discard the lemongrass pieces as you eat (they will be woody, but will have added a lovely aroma).

Easy Swap

Feel free to add extra protein in the form of tofu.

If you can't get hold of makrut lime leaves, use the zest of a lemon or lime instead.

You can also use flat rice noodles instead of vermicelli rice noodles – simply cook for 5–6 minutes.

STIR-FRIED NOODLES WITH VEGETABLES

(PAD MEE JAY)

Serves 4

Cooking time: 20 minutes

200g (7oz) dried flat rice noodles

2–3 tbsp vegetable oil

2 garlic cloves, finely chopped

1 block (about 390g/14oz) firm
tofu, patted dry with paper
towels and cut into 5mm (¼in)
slices

1 carrot, julienned

2 spring onions (scallions), sliced

½ sweetheart cabbage, thinly
sliced

Handful of beansprouts

Salt and ground white pepper

For the sauce

1–2 tbsp vegan oyster sauce

1 tbsp dark soy sauce

1–2 tbsp light soy sauce

1 tsp sugar

**My nan's signature dish and another childhood favourite of
mine, this stir-fried rice noodle dish is very popular during the
vegetarian festival in Thailand held around October each year.
My nan always made sure that we didn't cut the noodles up as
we ate, as it's considered bad luck!**

Cook the noodles in boiling water for 4–6 minutes until softened,
then drain and set aside.

Heat the oil in a frying pan or wok over a medium heat and add
the garlic. Fry for 1–2 minutes, until golden, then add the tofu and
fry for a further 1–2 minutes until lightly crispy.

Next, add all the vegetables and stir-fry for 5–6 minutes over
a medium heat.

Add the drained noodles and mix well.

Mix the sauce ingredients together in a bowl, then pour over the
noodles and toss well to coat, seasoning with salt and pepper.
Taste, adding more of the individual sauces if you like, then divide
between bowls.

Easy Swap
Feel free to use whatever noodles you have to hand.

STIR-FRIED MUSHROOMS WITH CHILLI AND THAI BASIL

(PAD HED BAI HORAPA)

Serves 4

Cooking time: 15 minutes

250g (9oz) mixed Asian mushrooms, such as shiitake, oyster, king oyster (eringi), shimeji or enoki

3 tbsp vegetable oil

2 garlic cloves, finely chopped

½ large red chilli, finely sliced

2 tbsp soy sauce

1 tbsp Thai sweet chilli sauce (see page 172 for homemade)

Handful of Thai basil

Ground black pepper

To serve
Perfect jasmine rice (page 168)

With very few ingredients, this is a quick and easy dish that is perfect for a midweek meal or busy day. Perfect with jasmine rice or riceberry.

Wipe the mushrooms clean with paper towels and remove the end part of the stalks. Cut into bite-sized pieces.

Heat the oil in a wok or frying pan over a medium heat, add the garlic and stir for 1–2 minutes until fragrant.

Add the mushrooms and stir-fry for 5 minutes. Add the chilli and season with the soy sauce and sweet chilli sauce. Add the Thai basil, toss quickly to combine and cook for 2–3 minutes. Garnish with pepper and serve with jasmine rice.

Easy Swap
You can also use any kind of mushrooms here – swap the Asian mushroom for hearty button or open cap mushrooms, or go meaty with sliced portobello.

GRILLED AUBERGINE WITH CHILLI AND COCONUT SAUCE

(YUM MA KEU MOUNG)

Serves 4 as a side dish

Cooking time: 25 minutes

2 large aubergines (eggplants), sliced 1.5cm (⅔in) thick

3–4 tbsp vegetable oil

Pinch each of salt and ground white pepper

For the sauce

2 tbsp Thai chilli jam (nam prik pao)

4 tbsp lime juice

2 tbsp vegan fish sauce or soy sauce

2 tbsp brown sugar

4 tbsp coconut milk

1 bird's eye chilli, finely chopped

1 tbsp toasted desiccated (dried shredded) coconut

1 tbsp finely sliced lemongrass stalk (outer layers removed, discard green part)

1 baby shallot, finely sliced

To finish

Handful of Thai basil leaves

Handful of coriander (cilantro) leaves, roughly chopped

Handful of mint leaves

1 tbsp toasted cashews

2 tbsp warm coconut milk

This is my take on a traditional dish that usually includes minced (ground) pork, but is here made with just aubergine (eggplant) instead, resulting a really flavoursome Thai-style salad dish.

Preheat the oven to 200°C/400°F/Gas 6.

Place the aubergine (eggplant) slices on a baking tray and brush the oil over both sides. Sprinkle with the salt and pepper and bake for 10–15 minutes until cooked and lightly browned.

Meanwhile, add all the sauce ingredients to a large bowl, mix well and set aside.

When the aubergines are cooked, add to the sauce bowl and use a large spoon to gently combine.

Add most of the herbs, reserving some to garnish, and gently mix again.

Arrange the aubergine on a platter, scraping out any dressing too, then top with the cashews and reserved herbs. Drizzle with the coconut milk and serve.

SPICY COCONUT BROTH WITH MUSHROOMS

(TOM KHA HED)

Serves 2

Cooking time: 20 minutes

1 x 400g (14oz) can of coconut milk

2 lemongrass stalks, outer layers removed, cut into 3cm (1¼in) lengths and bashed

2 thumb-sized pieces of galangal, peeled, thickly sliced (2cm/¾in) and bashed

3 makrut lime leaves, central woody stem removed, roughly chopped

3–4 bird's eye chillies

200g (7oz) oyster mushrooms (or chestnut or shiitake), cleaned and cut into bite-sized pieces

2 tbsp palm sugar or brown sugar

3–4 tbsp vegan fish sauce or soy sauce

2 tbsp tamarind paste

2 tbsp lime juice

Handful of coriander (cilantro), roughly chopped

To finish

1–2 tbsp chilli oil (optional)

1 tbsp thinly sliced red chilli

A hug-in-the-bowl type of soup; tasty and creamy but still light. Thai people like to add chicken to pair with the mushrooms, but it works beautifully with just mushrooms.

Bring the coconut milk to the boil in a large saucepan over a medium heat. When boiling, turn down to medium-low and add the lemongrass, galangal, lime leaves and chillies and stir well. Cook for 2–3 minutes.

Add the mushrooms and season with the sugar, fish sauce or soy sauce and tamarind. Stir well and simmer for a further 5 minutes.

Add the lime juice and most of the coriander (cilantro), reserving a little for a garnish.

Ladle into bowls, drizzle with a little chilli oil, if using, and garnish with the reserved coriander and the chilli.

Easy Swap
Swap galangal for ginger and use the zest of a lemon or lime in place of the makrut lime leaves.

sweet treats
THAI-STYLE

PUMPKIN IN COCONUT SYRUP

(FAK TONG BUAT)

Serves 4

Cooking time: 20 minutes, plus soaking

100–150g (3½–5oz) pumpkin or seasonal squash, peeled, deseeded and cut into small cubes

2–3 tbsp pickling lime/limestone, or 1 tbsp bicarbonate of soda (baking soda)

240ml (8fl oz/1 cup) water

1 x 400g (14oz) can of coconut milk

2 pandan leaves (optional)

150g (5oz) palm sugar or white sugar

1 tsp salt

To serve

1 tsp toasted sesame seeds (optional)

This is one of my favourite Thai desserts that my mum cooked a lot when we were young – so delicious and comforting. Soaking the pumpkin in a limestone solution (see page 10) firms it up so that it doesn't turn mushy when cooked. Do note that smaller pumpkins or squash will give sweeter results.

Place the pumpkin pieces in a bowl.

Dissolve the pickling lime/limestone (or bicarb/baking soda) in the water then wait for it to settle. Pour the clear part of the water over the pumpkin (you can save the lime solids that have settled at the bottom to use again), leave to soak for 30 minutes, then drain and rinse.

Add the coconut milk, pandan leaves, if using, and sugar to a saucepan. Place over a low heat and stir until the sugar has all dissolved.

Add the salt, then add the pumpkin.

Simmer over a medium heat for 12–15 minutes, until the pumpkin is soft.

Spoon into bowls and sprinkle with sesame seeds to serve, if you like.

PINEAPPLE SYRUP
WITH CRUSHED ICE

(SAPPAROD LOI KEAW)

Serves 2

**Cooking time: 15 minutes,
  plus cooling**

1 x 225g (8oz) can of pineapple
  pieces in juice

2 tbsp sugar

Crushed ice

6–8 grapes, peeled

**This dish consists of a delicious pineapple in syrup served with
crushed ice. Such a refreshing, light dessert.**

Add the pineapple and juice to a small saucepan with the sugar
and place over a medium heat. Stir until the sugar has dissolved
and the juice has started thickening, about 10 minutes, then take
off the heat and leave to cool.

Add some crushed ice to each serving bowl and top with the
pineapple, syrup and grapes.

Easy Swap
This works well with so many fruits – try swapping the pineapple
for canned mango, orange or peach.

STICKY RICE WITH MANGO

(KHAO NEAW MAMUANG)

Serves 4

Cooking time: 45 minutes, plus soaking and resting

250g (9oz) Thai sticky rice or glutinous rice

240ml (8fl oz/1 cup) coconut milk

2 pandan leaves (optional)

80g (3oz) granulated sugar

2–3 sweet, ripe mangos, peeled and thickly sliced

Salt

To serve

1 tbsp toasted sesame seeds or cooked yellow split mung beans

Mint leaves

This is a well-known Thai dessert that you have to try when on holiday in Thailand. It's actually really easy to make the sticky rice, then you just place some fresh mango slices over it and drizzle with salty creamy coconut sauce; heaven!

Rinse the rice in cold water a few times, then leave to soak for at least 2 hours, or overnight.

Drain the soaked rice and transfer to a muslin (cheesecloth). Fold the cloth loosely over the rice to cover and enclose. Place the rice in its cloth in a bamboo steamer (or any steamer you have). Cover and steam over a medium-high heat for about 15 minutes, then fold back the cloth and use a spatula to turn the rice over. Fold the cloth back over the rice and cook for a further 10 minutes, or until cooked.

Meanwhile, spoon 2 tablespoons of the thick coconut milk from the can into a small saucepan and place over a low heat, stirring continuously. Once it starts to simmer, add a pinch of salt, mix and take off the heat.

To make the sweet coconut sauce, put the remaining coconut milk in another saucepan, add the pandan leaves, if using, sugar and ½ teaspoon of salt, and stir until all the sugar has dissolved.

Once your sticky rice is cooked, transfer it to a large mixing bowl. Add the sweet coconut milk sauce and mix well. Rest for about 30 minutes to allow the rice to absorb all the sauce.

Serve with the mango and top with the salty coconut milk and toasted sesame seeds or cooked yellow split mung beans, and a few mint leaves to decorate, if you like.

Easy Swap
Pandan leaves add a lovely grassy flavour, but simply omit them if you can't find any.

You'll find yellow split mung beans in Asian supermarkets, but toasted sesame seeds here are lovely too.

BANANA FRITTERS

(GLUAY TOD)

Makes 6—8

Cooking time: 20 minutes

1 large banana, peeled and cut into 3cm (1¼in) chunks (you should get 6—8 pieces)

220ml (7½fl oz) vegetable oil

1 tbsp plain peanuts

3 tbsp maple syrup or honey

For the batter

2 tbsp plain (all-purpose) flour

2 tbsp cornflour (cornstarch)

1 tsp baking powder

Pinch of salt

Pinch of ground cinnamon

2 tbsp melted butter

2—3 tbsp limestone water (see page 10) or cold/soda water

This recipe is my take on a banana fritter called *kluay kaek*, a common Thai street food snack. These are super-crispy, crunchy, light and moreish and so easy to make.

Combine the batter ingredients in a mixing bowl and mix well until it is fully combined and there are no lumps. Add the banana pieces and gently mix with a spoon, making sure they're all coated in the batter.

Heat the oil in a small saucepan over a medium heat. When the oil is hot, add the banana pieces one at a time so they are evenly spaced in the pan (you will have to do this in batches) and shallow-fry for about 2—3 minutes, then turn them over and cook for another 2—3 minutes on the other side, until golden brown and crisp.

Remove the fritters from the pan and drain on a plate lined with paper towels.

In a clean pan over a medium heat, toast the peanuts for 2—3 minutes, tossing them occasionally, until pale brown. Transfer to a pestle and mortar and roughly crush.

Place the banana fritters on a plate, drizzle with the maple syrup or honey and sprinkle with toasted peanuts to serve.

Easy Swap

I use limestone water (see page 10) to make the batter extra crispy and to ensure the crispiness lasts longer, but if you can't find limestone water simply use cold water or soda water instead.

You can make these using pineapple instead of banana, or combine the two for a delicious duo fritter.

BANANA IN COCONUT SYRUP

(GLUAY BUAT CHEE)

Serves 4

Cooking time: 10 minutes

1 x 400g (14oz) can of coconut milk

100g (3½oz) sugar

2–3 pandan leaves (optional)

3–4 unripe bananas (with a greenish skin), peeled and cut into 4.5cm (1¾in) pieces

Pinch of salt

To serve
1 tsp toasted sesame seeds (optional)

This is one of my favourite childhood desserts, and one of the simplest puddings to cook at home. Every school canteen in Thailand serves this, so as you can imagine, I ate this countless times. Truly a hug in a bowl!

Add the coconut milk, sugar and pandan leaves, if using, to a small saucepan and simmer over a low heat for 5–6 minutes.

Add the bananas to the pan and gently stir for about 3 more minutes. Season with the salt and give it a quick stir until combined.

Serve warm, topped with toasted sesame seeds, if you like.

Easy Swap
You can replace the banana with sweet potato for a sweet and savoury dessert, just cook it for an extra 10 minutes or so to allow it to soften and cook through.

COCONUT ICE CREAM

(I-TIM KA TI)

Serves 2

Cooking time: 15 minutes, plus freezing

200ml (7fl oz) double (heavy) cream

130g (4½oz) caster (superfine) sugar

1 tsp salt

1 x 400g (14oz) can of coconut milk

20g (¾oz) honey

Authentic Thai coconut ice cream is a must for me every time I travel back to visit my family in Thailand, and it reminds me of a family day out at a floating market. It is really easy to make, especially now that canned coconut milk is widely available. As for what to serve it with, you can go fully traditional and serve it with sticky rice and mango (see page 156), or simply serve it on its own or in a cone. Or be more adventurous and go down the Thai street food route of serving a couple of scoops on top of a sweet brioche bun, topped with roasted crushed peanuts and condensed milk!

Using an electric whisk, beat the cream, sugar and salt together for about 10 minutes, until thick, then add the coconut milk and honey and beat again on a low speed for another 5 minutes.

Put the mixture into an ice-cream machine and churn for about 40 minutes, or following the manufacturer's instructions. Transfer to a freezerproof tub with lid and place in the freezer for about 6 hours or until set.

Easy Swap
If you don't have ice-cream machine, put the mixture into a tub, close the lid and put in the freezer for about an hour. After an hour, take it out and use a fork to stir the mixture around, then put back in the freezer. Repeat this every hour for 3–4 hours.

I use cream as well here, but you can easily make it dairy free by using extra coconut milk instead.

MELON BALLS AND SAGO IN COCONUT SYRUP

(MELON SAGO NAM KATI)

Serves 4

Cooking time: 25 minutes

½ small cantaloupe or honeydew melon

1 x 400g (14oz) can of coconut milk

1–2 pandan leaves (optional)

100g (3½oz) palm sugar or caster (superfine) sugar

1 tsp salt

80g (3oz) sago (or tapioca)

Crushed ice

Melon often pairs with coconut milk and tapioca or sago to make a refreshing and aromatic dessert in Southeast Asian countries, including Thailand. You can't beat a bowl of cool, refreshing melon balls and sago in coconut syrup on a warm summer's day. You can also try this warm when autumn comes, by leaving out the ice.

Scoop out all the melon seeds, then use a small scoop or melon baller to scoop the melon into balls. (You can also cut them into small cubes if you prefer.) Set aside.

Heat the coconut milk in a pan over a low heat, tie the pandan leaves, if using, into a knot and add them to the pan with the sugar. Stir until the sugar has dissolved, then add the salt. Mix well, remove from the heat and leave to cool.

Rinse the sago a few times in cold water and place in a clean saucepan. Add water to come just above the sago, and bring to the boil. Turn the heat down to medium-low and keep stirring gently until the sago turns translucent but still has a small white spot in the centre. Drain into a sieve (strainer) and run cold water through it for a few minutes, to prevent it from sticking together.

To serve, add some crushed ice to the bottom of each serving bowl, then spoon over some sago, coconut syrup and melon balls.

MINI COCONUT PANCAKES

(KHANOM BAA BIN)

Makes 20–25 mini pancakes

Cooking time: 25 minutes

100g (3½oz) desiccated (dried shredded) coconut

180ml (6fl oz) coconut milk, plus extra, if needed

150g (5oz) glutinous rice flour

20g (¾oz) cornflour (cornstarch)

120g (4¼oz) caster (superfine) sugar

1 tsp salt

Vegetable spray oil, for pan-frying

This is my all-time favourite sweet snack! In Thailand, you will see this dessert served as street food. This is my take.

Mix the coconut, coconut milk, glutinous rice flour, cornflour (cornstarch), sugar and salt together in a mixing bowl until combined. The mixture should be thick and not runny, but if it is too thick, you can add 2–3 tablespoons of water of coconut milk to loosen.

Spray some cooking oil over the base of a non-stick frying pan over a low heat. Add about 1 tablespoon of the pancake mixture to the pan and repeat with as many pancakes as you can fit at once in the pan, then let cook for 3–4 minutes before turning them over and cooking the other side for another 2–3 minutes.

Repeat to use up all the batter. Enjoy with tea or coffee.

sides, sauces & PASTES

PERFECT JASMINE RICE

Serves 4

250g (9oz) Thai jasmine rice
About 400ml (14fl oz/1⅔ cups) water

Rinse the rice in cold water a few times until the water is clear, to get rid of some of the starch.

Place in a small pan and add the water (or put your finger on top of the rice surface – the water level should come to about the first knuckle line of your index finger).

Place, uncovered, over a high heat for 8–10 minutes, until the rice has started to absorb the water. Turn the heat down to the lowest setting, put the lid on and let cook for 5–8 minutes, until the rice has completely absorbed the water and the grains are sitting individually.

Remove from the heat and leave, covered, to finish cooking off the heat for a further 10 minutes.

THAI STICKY RICE

Serves 4

250g (9oz) Thai sticky rice or glutinous rice

Rinse the rice in cold water a few times, then leave to soak for at least 2 hours, or overnight.

Drain the soaked rice and transfer to a muslin (cheesecloth). Fold the cloth loosely over the rice to cover and enclose.

Place the rice in its cloth in a bamboo steamer (or any steamer you have). Cover and steam over a medium-high heat for about 15 minutes, then fold back the cloth and use a spatula to turn the rice over. Fold the cloth back over the rice and cook for a further 10 minutes, or until cooked.

TOASTED GROUND RICE
(KHAO KHUA)

Makes about 45g (1½oz)

4–5 tbsp Thai jasmine rice

Toasted ground rice gives dishes a smokiness and a nuttiness. It is often added in northeastern and Isan-style dishes, such as spicy laab (see page 47), in the dipping sauce nam jim jaew (see page 170) and in Thai jungle curry (see page 96) to thicken up the sauce.

Add the rice to a dry pan over a medium-high heat and stir constantly until it is toasted and becoming dark brown and fragrant.

Transfer the toasted rice to a pestle and mortar or spice grinder and pound or grind until it turns into a powder.

Store in a cool, dark place in an airtight jar for up to 6 months.

NAM JIM JAEW

(SPICY THAI ISAN DIPPING SAUCE)

Makes a small bowlful

4 garlic cloves, unpeeled

3 baby shallots, unpeeled

2 bird's eye chillies

1 tbsp toasted ground rice (see page 169)

1 tsp tamarind paste

1 tbsp palm sugar or brown sugar

Juice of 1 lime (2–3 tbsp)

2 tbsp fish sauce

1 tbsp finely chopped coriander (cilantro)

1 tbsp dried chilli flakes

This smoky, spicy dipping sauce is served with Thai-style BBQ dishes or grilled meats, such as crying tiger (see page 65), chicken wings or BBQ pork. Every household or food vendor has their own recipe and method, and here is mine.

Place the garlic, shallots and chillies in a dry frying pan and toast over a medium heat for 15 minutes, stirring occasionally until nicely toasted and golden brown. (Alternatively, wrap in foil, place on a baking tray and roast for 15 minutes in a 180°C/350°F/ Gas 4 oven.)

When cool enough to handle, peel off the garlic and shallot skins.

Transfer to a pestle and mortar or blender and pound or process to a smooth paste.

Transfer to a bowl and mix in the toasted ground rice, tamarind paste, palm sugar, lime juice and fish sauce.

Add the coriander (cilantro) and chilli flakes and mix well. This will keep in a lidded jar in the fridge for 2–3 days.

Pictured overleaf.

PRIK NAM SOM

(CHILLI VINEGAR)

Makes a small bowlful

5 large red chillies (any variety), roughly chopped

3–4 garlic cloves, peeled

240ml (8fl oz/1 cup) white vinegar

1 tsp sugar

This well-known spicy Thai condiment is served with many noodle dishes, and is perfect for adding to noodle soups. Thai people love adding it to give the noodles an extra lift of heat and sourness.

Add the chillies and garlic to a blender or pestle and mortar and blend or pound until combined into a fine paste.

Add the vinegar and sugar and mix well.

Transfer to a small bowl to serve. Stored in a lidded jar in the fridge, it will keep for 2–3 days.

Pictured overleaf.

NAM JIM SEAFOOD SAUCE

Here is another spicy dipping sauce that reminds me of Thai beach holidays, and is a must-have when you order seafood dishes in Thailand. This is great for spooning over a seafood platter.

Makes a small bowlful

6–8 green bird's eye chillies

1 tbsp sea salt

2 garlic cloves, peeled

Juice of 1½ limes (3–4 tbsp)

2 tbsp sugar

1 tbsp coriander (cilantro) root, finely chopped

Pound the ingredients together in a pestle and mortar. It should taste salty, sour, spicy and sweet. Alternatively, place all the ingredients in a blender and process to a lightly thick sauce.

Transfer to a small bowl to serve. Stored in a lidded jar in the fridge, it will keep for 2–3 days.

THAI SWEET CHILLI SAUCE

This is a must-have dipping sauce with so many Thai dishes, such as spring rolls, pork patties, and more.

Makes about 300ml (10fl oz)

10 large red chillies

6–8 garlic cloves, chopped

150ml (5fl oz/⅔ cup) white vinegar

240ml (8fl oz/1 cup) water

2 tbsp salt

250g (9oz) caster (superfine) sugar

2 tbsp cornflour (cornstarch) mixed with 4 tbsp water

Blitz the chillies, garlic and vinegar in a blender, then transfer the mixture to a saucepan.

Add the water, salt and sugar and bring to a boil.

Add the cornflour (cornstarch) mixture and keep stirring until the sauce thickens. Take off the heat and leave to cool.

Transfer to a clean, sterilized bottle or jar with a lid and store for up to 3 months. Once opened, store in the fridge and use within 2 weeks.

NAM PLA PRIK

PRIK NAM SOM

NAM JIM SEAFOOD SAUCE

NAM JIM JAEW

THAI SWEET CHILLI SAUCE

AR JARD

AR JARD

Makes a small bowlful

8 tbsp caster (superfine) sugar

6 tbsp rice vinegar

Pinch of salt

2 tbsp water

5cm (2in) piece of cucumber

1 shallot, halved and finely sliced

1 large red chilli, finely sliced

Popularly served alongside many Thai dishes, this refreshing cucumber relish is sweet, sour and salty with a hint of spiciness coming through. We often serve it with Thai fish cakes, spring rolls, Thai pork on toast, sweetcorn fritters and crispy pancakes.

Place the sugar and vinegar in a small pan and place over a medium-high heat. Add the salt and water and stir well. Once it starts to bubble, take off the heat and leave to cool.

Peel the cucumber (I use a julienne peeler for its pretty effect but a swivel peeler is fine) and cut in half lengthwise. Use a small spoon to scoop out the seeds and, if the cucumber is on the fatter side, cut in half again. Slice into thin half (or quarter) moons.

Pour the cooled liquid into a bowl and add the slices of cucumber, shallot and chilli. Serve immediately.

Pictured on page 173.

NAM PLA PRIK

Makes a small bowlful

4–5 bird's eye chillies, finely chopped (or more if you prefer extra heat)

Juice of 2 limes (3–4 tbsp)

8–10 tbsp fish sauce

1 tsp brown sugar

2 garlic cloves, finely sliced

An essential dipping sauce in Thai cuisine that showcases how Thai food is all about the balance of sour, salty, sweet and spicy. The amount of chilli is easily changed to suit your taste. Delicious served with lots of Thai food, such a pad krapow (stir-fried chilli, garlic and basil), crispy Thai crispy omelette, stir-fried rice, and much more. Double or triple the quantities and store any excess in a covered container in the fridge for up to 7 days.

Put all the ingredients into a bowl and mix.

Pictured on page 173.

THAI CURRY PASTE REFERENCE CHART

	Red curry	Green curry	Panang curry	Massaman curry
Dried red chilli	•		•	•
Fresh red chilli	•	•	•	•
Fresh green chilli		•		
Garlic	•	•	•	•
Shrimp paste	•	•	•	•
Shallot	•	•	•	•
Coriander / cilantro roots	•	•	•	•
Galangal	•	•	•	•
Lemongrass	•	•	•	•
Makrut lime zest	•	•	•	•
Ground coriander	•	•	•	•
Ground white pepper	•	•	•	•
Salt	•	•	•	•
Ground cumin		•	•	•
Ground cloves			•	•
Star anise				•
Ground cinnamon				•
Fresh turmeric				
Ground peanuts			•	
Lesser galangal				

	Yellow curry	Jungle curry	Thai sour curry	Khao soi curry	Thai clear curry
Dried red chilli	•		•	•	
Fresh red chilli	•	•	•		
Fresh green chilli					
Garlic	•	•	•	•	•
Shrimp paste	•	•	•	•	•
Shallot	•	•	•	•	•
Coriander / cilantro roots					•
Galangal	•	•		•	
Lemongrass		•		•	
Makrut lime zest				•	
Ground coriander		•			
Ground white pepper					•
Salt	•	•	•	•	•
Ground cumin					
Ground cloves					
Star anise					
Ground cinnamon					
Fresh turmeric	•			•	
Ground peanuts					
Lesser galangal		•			

CURRY PASTES

Here are all the Thai curry pastes featured in the book for you to refer back to. For each, simply pound all the ingredients in a pestle and mortar until you have a rough paste. Alternatively, add all the ingredients to a food processor and pulse until you acheive a paste. Stored in a lidded jar in the fridge, these pastes will keep for 1–2 weeks.

Each of the ingredients has its own specific flavour and aroma, so these easy swaps won't yield as authentic a result – but if you can't find the original ingredients, replace with the below.

Easy Swaps

- Use regular lime or lemon zest instead of makrut lime zest.

- Use red onions instead of shallots.

- Use ginger instead of galangal or lesser galangal.

- Use miso paste instead of shrimp paste to make these vegan- or vegetarian-friendly.

THAI GREEN CURRY PASTE

Makes about 1 cup (enough for 6–8 servings)

25 green bird's eye chillies
4 large fresh red chillies
1 tbsp shrimp paste (or use miso paste to make vegan)
5 garlic cloves, chopped
5 baby shallots, finely sliced
1 tbsp finely sliced coriander (cilantro) roots
1 tbsp finely sliced galangal
1 tbsp finely sliced lemongrass
1 tsp chopped makrut lime zest
1 tsp ground white pepper
1 tsp ground coriander
1 tsp ground cumin
1 tsp salt
Handful of Thai basil (optional)

PANANG CURRY PASTE

Makes about 1 cup (enough for 6–8 servings)

5 large dried red chillies, sliced
8 large fresh red chillies, sliced
1 tbsp shrimp paste (or use miso paste to make vegan)
5 garlic cloves, chopped
5 baby shallots, finely sliced
1 tbsp finely sliced coriander (cilantro) roots
1 tbsp finely sliced galangal
1 tbsp finely sliced lemongrass
1 tsp chopped makrut lime zest
1 tsp ground white pepper
1 tsp ground coriander
1 tsp ground cumin
2 tbsp peanuts
1 tsp salt

THAI RED CURRY PASTE

Makes about 1 cup (enough for 6–8 servings)

5 large dried red chillies, sliced

8 large fresh red chillies, sliced

1 tbsp shrimp paste (or use miso paste to make vegan)

5 garlic cloves, chopped

5 baby shallots, finely sliced

1 tbsp finely sliced coriander (cilantro) roots

1 tbsp finely sliced galangal

1 tbsp finely sliced lemongrass

1 tsp chopped makrut lime zest

1 tsp ground white pepper

1 tsp ground coriander

1 tsp salt

JUNGLE CURRY PASTE

Makes about 1 cup (enough for 6–8 servings)

20 red bird's eye chillies, sliced

1 tbsp shrimp paste (or use miso paste to make vegan)

3 garlic cloves, chopped

5 baby shallots, finely sliced

1 tbsp finely sliced galangal

1 tbsp finely sliced lemongrass

1 tsp ground coriander

1 tsp salt

1 tbsp shredded lesser galangal (see page 10)

MASSAMAN CURRY PASTE

Makes about 1 cup (enough for 6–8 servings)

5 large dried red chillies, sliced

8 large fresh red chillies, sliced

1 tbsp shrimp paste (or use miso paste to make vegan)

5 garlic cloves, chopped

5 baby shallots, finely sliced

1 tbsp coriander (cilantro) roots, finely sliced

1 tbsp finely sliced galangal

1 tbsp finely sliced lemongrass

1 tsp chopped makrut lime zest

1 tsp ground white pepper

1 tsp ground coriander

1 tsp ground cumin

1 star anise

1 tsp ground cinnamon

1 tsp ground cloves

1 tsp salt

YELLOW CURRY PASTE

Makes about 1 cup (enough for 6–8 servings)

5 large dried red chillies, sliced

8 large fresh red chillies, sliced

1 tbsp shrimp paste (or use miso paste to make vegan)

5 garlic cloves, chopped

5 baby shallots, finely sliced

1 tbsp finely sliced galangal

2 thumb-sized pieces of fresh turmeric, finely sliced

1 tsp salt

THAI CURRY PASTE REFERENCE CHART

PANANG CURRY PASTE

MASSAMAN CURRY PASTE

RED CURRY PASTE

YELLOW CURRY PASTE

THAI GREEN CURRY PASTE

NAM PRIK KA PI (PAGE 127)

JUNGLE CURRY PASTE

THAI SOUR CURRY PASTE

Makes about ½ cup (enough for 3–4 servings)

5 large dried red chillies, sliced

8 large fresh red chillies, sliced

1 tbsp shrimp paste (or use miso paste to make vegan)

5 garlic cloves, chopped

5 baby shallots, finely sliced

1 tsp salt

KHAO SOI CURRY PASTE

Makes about ½ cup (enough for 3–4 servings)

10 large dried red chillies, sliced

2 tbsp shrimp paste (or use miso paste to make vegan)

5 garlic cloves, chopped

5 baby shallots, finely sliced

1 tbsp finely sliced galangal

1 tbsp finely sliced lemongrass

1 tsp chopped makrut lime zest

1 thumb-sized piece of fresh turmeric, finely sliced

1 tsp salt

THAI CLEAR CURRY PASTE

Makes about ½ cup (enough for 3–4 servings)

1 tbsp ground white pepper

2 tbsp shrimp paste (or use miso paste to make vegan)

1 tbsp sliced fresh coriander (cilantro) roots

4 garlic cloves, chopped

2 baby shallots, chopped

1 tsp salt

MEAL PLANS FOR ALL OCCASIONS

Thai people do not eat just one dish, we have a series of dishes that complement and contrast with each other. For example, one meal for a typical Thai evening would be a spicy dish, soup, stir-fry and a sweet and sour dish, all served together. We called this *sum rup*.

Here are some *sum rup* ideas for your meal plan, with dishes that go together well so you can enjoy the experience of Thai meals even more.

Simple dinner with family: Stir-fried prawns with holy basil and chilli (see page 54), Sweetcorn fritters (see page 31), Beef massaman curry (see page 93), Stir-fried chicken and ginger (see page 118).

Midweek dinner: Stir-fried asparagus with prawns in oyster sauce (see page 104), stir-fried rice, Thai crispy omelette (see page 116), Panang beef curry (see page 88).

Weekend at home: Thai Pork patties (see page 29), Spicy sweetcorn salad (see page 48), Thai green curry (see page 82), Sweet and sour veg with chicken (see page 113).

Casual friends over: Choo chee curry with salmon (see page 90), King prawns in blankets (see page 24), Thai chicken satay (see page 22), Spring rolls (see page 34), Spicy glass noodle salad (see page 40), Thai fried rice with crab (see page 78).

Cook to impress: Tom yum kuung (see page 60), Pad Thai kuung sod (see page 66), Salmon waterfall salad (see page 42), Thai railway fried rice (see page 57), My grandma's sticky pork belly (see page 114).

Something special: Crying tiger (see page 65), Spicy papaya salad (see page 77), Thai sticky rice (see page 168), Duck in red curry (see page 91), Pan-fried salmon (see page 124), Perfect jasmine rice (see page 168).

INDEX

THANK YOU

From the bottom of my heart, I extend massive thanks to my family in both Thailand and the UK. To my dad, Khun Por Pornchai, and my mum, Khun Mea Tassanee, for the pure love and inspiration you have given me throughout my life. To my sister Ton and my brother Chat, thank you for all the lovely memories that we have created and shared together.

To the most important people in my life, my husband Dan and my son Joe. You – both of you – are my everything, always believing in me and being there for me. Thank you for being such enthusiastic eaters, and for tasting my food for the past 20-odd years without complaint. I love you more than words can describe.

Thank you to my mother- and father-in-law Chris and John for your tireless support. I am so proud to be your daughter-in-law. Cheers to many more Thai green curries and massaman curries!

Big thanks to all my lovely friends – you are my extended family; to my giggling girls gang, my friends for life gang and my dance workout gang, for being there for me and supporting me every step of the way. Many thanks, too, to all my Thai friends – my friends forever gang and my friends from RWB high school and university. Every time I visit Thailand we meet up to share good Thai food and have a great laugh. I am so grateful.

Thank you to everyone who has been to my cooking classes, both in person and on Zoom, as well as those who have been to my cooking demos and to all the lovely clients that I have cooked for! A big shout out to my lovely agent, Nikki. I am grateful to meet friends wherever I go, from the UK to Australia to Thailand to Malaysia. Thank you to my social media friends and fans – it makes my day every time you try out my recipes and tag me.

There would never have been even a cookbook without you... Thank you, Quadrille publishing team who believed in me from the start, with special thanks to Harriet, Sofie and Alicia. I still remember the moment when I first read the email reply from you. I read it again and again in disbelief with happy tears. The journey from dreaming of one day having my own cookbook to finally making one is so special and I cannot thank you enough! Thank you, too, to all the people behind the scenes for bringing this to life, including food stylist and assistant, prop stylist, and food photographer – thank you to Sam, Charlie and Luke who have worked so closely with me to make this book so inviting and beautiful.

For me, my mum, my aunt and both of my nans are the most inspiring people in my life, who have motivated me to grow and believe in myself. My mum taught me that hard times can be overcome and that losing battles can be won. 'You can do better next time, so learn from your mistakes,' she always said. These two women have taught me more about cooking than I could have learned from any cookbook. My biggest thank-you of all goes to my beloved mum who is no longer with us. Her food was so special because she put her love and care into every dish she cooked. She taught and showed me what good food is. She will always be with me in my heart.

I hope my mum is looking down on me, that she is proudly saying 'That's my darling girl!'

ABOUT THE AUTHOR

Yui Miles comes from a Thai-Chinese family where cooking and eating have always been a key focus of daily life. She learned how to cook from a young age, from her mum and the knowledge of her aunt, who was a chef in the Thai royal kitchen. In 2001 she moved to the UK and brought her cooking talents with her. With her passion and skill she was able to secure a spot on *Masterchef UK* 2019, reaching the quarter finals, and also appeared on and won *Beat the Chef* on Channel 4. She has engaged Instagram where she shares her recipes, and now works as a cookery teacher, recipe creator and private chef. This is her first book.

Managing Director Sarah Lavelle

Commissioning Editor Harriet Webster

Assistant Editor Sofie Shearman

Copy Editor Sally Somers

Designer Alicia House

Cover Illustration Jordan Amy Lee

Photographer Luke Albert

Food Stylist Sam Dixon

Prop Stylist Charlie Phillips

Head of Production Stephen Lang

Senior Production Controller Katie Jarvis

First published in 2023 by Quadrille Publishing Limited

Quadrille
52–54 Southwark Street
London SE1 1UN
quadrille.com

Reprinted in 2023, 2024 (twice)
10 9 8 7 6 5 4

ISBN: 978 1 78713 994 7

Printed in China